PATRIOT JOHN

The Man Who Saved America

Philip B. Secor

HERITAGE BOOKS
2005

HERITAGE BOOKS

AN IMPRINT OF HERITAGE BOOKS, INC.

Books, CDs, and more – Worldwide

For our listing of thousands of titles see our website
at
www.HeritageBooks.com

Published 2005 by
HERITAGE BOOKS, INC.
Publishing Division
65 East Main Street
Westminster, Maryland 21157-5026

Copyright © 2005 Philip B. Secor

Cover illustration:
"The Capture of Major André" by Thomas Sully
Courtesy of the Worcester Art Museum, Worcester, Massachusetts

International Standard Book Number: **0-7884-4088-8**

— CONTENTS —

— ILLUSTRATIONS —

— PREFACE —

My purpose in this book is to retell one of the most important and exciting stories in American history and, in the process, to restore one of our long-forgotten heroes to his rightful place in the country's collective memory. For a century after the event that secured this great man's reputation, he was hailed as one of the saviors of the American Republic. Statues, medals, parades, books, ballads and dramatic performances all bespoke the high esteem in which he was held by his fellow Americans, as did counties, towns, streets and schools named in his honor. He was known throughout America as "Patriot John."

I first heard the bare outlines of the tale from my mother when I was a small boy. She learned it from her grandmother, who was only doing her part to pass along memories of a famous ancestor from one generation to the next. Over the years, others have given me memorabilia that have helped to fill out my mother's accounting of a family legend that happens also to be a vital part of the American saga.

I am indebted to many historians, living and dead, whose works I have drawn upon and who have pointed me to important primary sources. Principal among these are James Flexner, Carl Van Doren, Thomas Jones, John Walsh, Lincoln Diamont, Richard Koke, Willard Wallace and Emma Patterson. Three near contemporaries of the hero of this story, his cousin the renowned writer James Kirke Paulding, the more famous James Fennimore Cooper and Abraham Boyce, a neighbor who shared some of his experiences, have left accounts which, although sometimes fictionalized, are invaluable for understanding the context of our hero's exploits.

Also helpful have been Sara Mascia, Curator at the Tarrytown Historical Society and my daughter and editor, Nanette Secor Smith of Atlanta, Georgia. I am especially grateful to Nan who took time from her many other editorial assignments to help her father. Roxanne Carlson of Flintlock Press has been unfailingly thoughtful and helpful during the final stages of publication.

Finally, I once again thank my best friend and wife, Anne, who is my constant companion and patient critic as I sally forth on adventures in search of forgotten heroes.[1]

[1] My other major attempt to restore a truly great man who had been forgotten is my biography of Richard Hooker, the sixteenth century founder of the Anglican religious tradition: *Richard Hooker Prophet of Anglicanism*, Burns & Oates/Continuum, London. 2001.

— PROLOGUE —

On September 23, 1780, a solitary rider reined in his horse at a bridge spanning a small river just north of the village of Tarrytown, New York. He had been riding all day and needed a brief rest before continuing on to his destination at nearby White Plains.

The horseman was keenly aware that the future of the American struggle for independence was riding with him. Soon he would be hailed as a hero. Just a few more miles to go and it would all be over.

Meanwhile, two other men were pursing their own dreams of glory on this September afternoon. The lives of these three would soon become inextricably linked in an incredible drama that would seal their fates and that of the fledgling American Republic.

Just a few more miles...

The Hudson Valley:
"Cockpit" of the Revolution

The Hudson River Valley of New York has been aptly called the "cockpit" of the American Revolution. The Americans needed to hold this area if they were to win their independence and the British had to control it if they were to put down the rebellion and retain their valuable colonies. Dutch settlers, including the Paulding family, which will figure importantly in our story, had lived in the valley for a hundred years and were used to being at the center of international conflict.[2] Their European homeland in the Low Countries had long been known as the "cockpit" of Europe because its location at the crossroads of trade and commerce had made it a battleground in the perpetual struggles among the nations of Europe.

The River

In a day when most long distance travel was by boat, the coastal waters and rivers of the American colonies provided the essential routes for both trade and warfare. The Hudson River was especially critical because it effectively joined the northern and the southern colonies by providing New England and the South access to one another as well as to the vital middle colonies.

Just as the river joined the colonies for purposes of commercial and military transport, so, during the Revolutionary War, it could potentially weaken the side that lost control of it.

---

[2] For a detailed account of the Paulding family in the Hudson Valley, see the *Appendix*.

Keenly aware of this tactical reality, George Washington wrote in a letter of early December 1777 to General Israel Putnam, his commander at Peekskill, that "the possession of [the Hudson] is indispensably essential to...communication between the Eastern, Middle and Southern States; and upon its security depends the flow of our chief supplies for the subsistence of [our]...forces." Thomas Jefferson echoed this sentiment, arguing that British control of the Hudson would "cut off all correspondence between the Northern and Southern colonies." General Philip Schuyler, Washington's commander of the Northern Army, said in a similar vein, "To me...every object, as to importance, sinks almost to nothing, when put in competition with the securing of Hudson's River."[3]

In July of 1776 a special secret committee of the New York Assembly was charged with developing and implementing strategies for defending the river and the valley. The legislature ordered that forts should be built and other means employed "that shall appear to [the committee] most effectual for obstructing the channel of Hudson's River or annoying the enemy's ships in their navigation up the said River." The committee met secretly with General Washington to plan strategy. Virtually everything that was subsequently done to defend the Hudson was the work of this small group of patriots which included notables such as: Robert Livingston, a member of the Continental Congress and one of the drafters of the Declaration of Independence; John Jay, then a young lawyer from Westchester County and later one of the authors of the famed *Federalist Papers* and, later still, the first Chief Justice of the U.S. Supreme Court; and William Paulding, a prosperous merchant of Dutch ancestry who had homes and commercial dealings both in New York City and in the small river settlement of Tarrytown about twenty-five miles upriver.

The long-range plan developed by Paulding and his colleagues involved building substantial forts along the riverbanks with large cannons trained on passing ships, especially in the highlands some

---

[3] These quotations are cited from Lincoln Diamont, *Chaining the Hudson: The Fight for the River in the American Revolution*, New York, 1989, xiii, 9. See also Alice Kenney, *Stubborn for Liberty: The Dutch in New York*, New York, 1975, 51-67.

forty miles north of New York City. In the meantime, several other methods were employed to secure the river including a constant campaign of harassment and disruption of English ships in New York Harbor. One tactic was to set afire empty boats and try to ram and sink enemy ships with them. Another method was to employ an early version of the submarine called "the turtle." This ingenious device, invented by William Bushnell, was designed to submerge in the harbor to ram and sink ships. The submarine did not work and the other strategies were only a minor annoyance to the English.

Another of the defenses of the Hudson involved linking old ships to span the river at narrow points just north of New York Harbor, especially at Fort Lee and Fort Washington. In the spaces between the ships great concrete blocks called *chevaus de-frise*, or "concrete horses" were sunk with long pointed spears jutting up from them just a few feet beneath the surface. These proved ineffective. The British easily breached them and took both forts in November of 1776 forcing Washington to abandon the river and retreat to Trenton.

A more successful short-term defense of the river involved stretching gigantic chains constructed of logs, concrete blocks, iron or a combination of these materials from shore to shore between sunken ships. The first of these giant chains was built in mid-1776 just south of West Point between Fort Montgomery on the west shore and Fort Clinton on the east bank. The following year another chain was strung across the river between an island near Beacon on one shore and Plum Island near the other. In April of 1778 a giant chain was stretched between West Point and Constitution Island. These barriers effectively blocked the British from sailing northward from that point for the rest of the war, although they continued to operate with impunity on the river south of this barrier, between Peekskill, New York, and New York City.

Throughout 1778 and 1779 the building of permanent fortifications on the highlands overlooking the river at and near West Point continued. In August 1779, General Benedict Arnold would take command of West Point and be personally involved in inspecting and repairing the famous chain across the Hudson. (An apocryphal story was later told of how he had secretly removed one of the links in the chain as part of his treason.) [4]

British Strategies

The English, of course, were no less sanguine about the Hudson than the Americans. Speaking retrospectively of the importance of the river to an English victory, General Clinton wrote in his *Memoirs*:

> The five North American governments to the eastward of Hudson's River teemed with a robust and hearty race of men seated in a mountainous and strongly defensible country. The Southern provinces were alone capable of furnishing the necessary supplies for the war. And these two districts were separated from each other by the River Hudson forming a broad navigable communication for 170 miles between New York and Albany. The Hudson naturally presented itself as a very important object.

Clinton went on to state that if he could have controlled the Hudson River, these two sections of America would have been unable to supply one another with essential food, troops and military supplies and he would then have been able to link his armies in Canada and New York, thereby assuring his military victory.[5] In fact, a plan employing the Hudson as a conduit for winning the war was presented to King George III in the winter of 1776 by one of his most celebrated officers, General John Burgoyne. The plan was to bring his army south from Montreal to the Hudson by way of Lake Champlain and Lake George and to meet General William Howe who would come upriver from New York City. These two armies would meet near Fort Orange (Albany) and henceforth control the Hudson—and thus the country.

The King approved the plan. Burgoyne set out from Canada in June of 1777 with an army of more than 7,000 regulars augmented

---

[4] The best description of these attempts to fortify the Hudson is Diamant, op. cit.

[5] Ibid., xiii-xiv.

along the route by some 400 German mercenaries and about 300 Canadian Tories and Native Americans. On July 6, he easily took Fort Ticonderoga on the northern shore of Lake Champlain but was later slowed in his advance by stiff resistance from Ethan Allen's Green Mountain Boys at Bennington, Vermont.[6] In late September, Burgoyne, by now meeting increasingly fierce resistance from the aroused locals, had encamped just north of Fort Orange to await the anticipated arrival of General Howe from New York.

Unfortunately for the English strategy, Howe and his officers were far more cautious than the daring "Gentleman Jack "Burgoyne.[7] They put too much emphasis on sketchy (and inaccurate) intelligence that exaggerated the strength of American fortifications. Belatedly, in June of 1777, Howe's general, Sir Henry Clinton, proceeded northward, meeting little resistance from the inadequate colonial fortifications along the river, and rather easily took Forts Clinton and Montgomery in the Highlands just south of West Point, as well as colonial garrisons at Stony Point and Verplanck Point. Clinton even took the substantial base at Peekskill commanded by the aging General Israel Putnam, the popular hero of Bunker Hill. On October 6, Clinton took Fort Constitution and sailed on upriver destroying rebel supplies and colonial homes and farms en route.

But it was all to no avail. Before Clinton reached the encamped Burgoyne to complete the decisive joining of English forces, the rebel generals, Benedict Arnold and Horatio Gates had come northward from their base at Morristown, New Jersey, to engage him. On October 7, the fierce and fateful battle of Saratoga began. When the fighting ended ten days later, the vastly superior colonial army of some 20,000 men had decisively defeated

---

[6] In about 1770 in the "green mountains" of what later became Vermont, Ethan Allen formed a band of fighters to resist efforts by New York to incorporate the region into their colony. Popularly known as the Green Mountain Boys, this band fought in several crucial engagements during the Revolution.

[7] The nickname "Gentleman Jack" stems from Burgoyne's varied career as Member of Parliament, successful playwright, valiant field commander in America and Portugal and vibrant outspoken style as a colorful and usually successful public figure of the day.

Burgoyne's outnumbered force which had to stand alone without the expected reinforcement from Clinton. On October 17, Burgoyne surrendered his entire army, still numbering more than 5,000 men, to Gates. It was to be the most decisive American victory in the war. As a result France, England's historic enemy, now decided the colonists had a chance to win their independence and moved quickly to help them do it.

When Clinton heard of Burgoyne's defeat, he retreated down the river, abandoning all that he had gained to the Americans—a critical mistake. General Washington and his staff moved quickly to fortify the highlands at and near West Point in order to assure their control of the Hudson River and valley north of New York City. In 1778, fortifications were begun in earnest at West Point, Verplanck Point, Stony Point and Fort Lafayette. By late spring of 1779 construction and manning of all of these fortifications were well underway, just in time to meet Clinton's new foray up river with 5,000 men in seventy ships. This time Clinton secured most of Westchester County and established a major base at White Plains.

In July, Washington sent General Anthony Wayne to recapture Stony Point. With great stealth and courage, "Mad Anthony," as he was thereafter known, was able to storm the fortification and capture over 500 men. Washington soon thereafter decided it was not worth keeping the fort and abandoned it. For his part, Clinton concluded that his recently captured Fort Lafayette wasn't worth fighting for and abandoned it to turn his attention to other theaters of war. The result of all this back and forth on the Hudson in 1778-79 was that each side now laid effective claim to a portion of the Hudson River Valley: the English controlling the lower part that ran from New York Harbor as far north as White Plains and the Americans the much larger part that ran northward from Peekskill to Albany and beyond.

— CHAPTER 2 —

The Neutral Ground

The area between the American and English lines—the so-called "neutral ground"—comprised some 22,000 inhabitants living mostly in and around a host of tiny hamlets and larger towns like Dobbs Ferry and Tarrytown on the Hudson, New Rochelle, Mamaroneck, and Rye on Long Island Sound, and Scarsdale, White Plains, Pound Ridge, Bedford, Mount Kisco and Peekskill in the interior. Not surprisingly, the ancestors of the Dutch settlers, who had inhabited this area for over a century, were not happy to be overrun by English invaders. Their characteristic qualities of rugged independence and provincial loyalty fused with an historic antagonism to English power that dated from sixteenth century struggles between England and Holland in Europe. Although tolerant of differences of opinion in religion and politics, they were fiercely resistant to both the invaders from Britain and those among their neighbors whose lineage was English and who now supported the Tory effort to crush American independence.[8]

Many of these Dutch-American farmers, who had long lived peaceably in the Hudson Valley, now waged a kind of guerilla warfare with some of their English-American neighbors in the neutral ground. Their strategy of looting, burning property and even killing local Tory sympathizers was retaliated in kind by many of their neighbors who opposed American independence and conducted raids on rebel militia and civilians. An intermittent civil war was waged in this dangerous zone between the lines. Many

---

[8] An excellent discussion of this civil war that raged in the neutral zone is in Henry M. Ward's *Between the Lines,* New York, 2002, esp. ix, 17-27. See also, Emma L. Patterson, *Peekskill in the American Revolution,* Peekskill, NY, 1944, 79-85; Kenney, op. cit., 159-60.

English sympathizers abandoned their homes fleeing southward behind the safety of British-held territory. Much of the area became a barren and dangerous wasteland of ruined houses, devastated fields and marauding bands of opportunists and outlaws.

Cowboys and Other Terrorists

Prominent among the bands of Tory loyalists who terrorized citizens in the neutral ground was the Queen's Raiders, led by one Robert Rogers; another was the Associated Raiders under Edmund Fanning; but the most feared was the Corps of Loyalist Refugees, popularly called the Cowboys. This large band of some 500 guerilla soldiers, some mounted and some on foot, was drawn mostly from local residents and led by about fifty horsemen who were members of the local English militia under the command of General Tryon. The footmen were dressed in their own civilian clothes, but the horsemen wore distinctive brown leggings and green coats faced with white supplied by the British.

The so-called Cowboys were often motivated not so much by loyalty to England as by a desire for revenge against those patriot neighbors who had stolen from them or even driven them from their homes. Although usually not paid for their service to the Crown, they fully intended that a portion of their stolen booty would not be turned over to the British army but kept as their own. Along the way, they often pillaged, burned, raped and killed. They were so despised by the residents that after the war a number of them were summarily shot to death on sight by their former neighbors in Westchester County.

By late 1780 the Cowboys were being led by James DeLancey who had been the sheriff of Westchester County before the war. Grandson of a former royal governor of New York and nephew of the chief justice of the New York Court (his namesake), DeLancey led the Cowboys on countless raids for several years. After the war, when called to account for his deeds, DeLancey claimed that the worst of what he was accused of had actually been perpetrated by common criminals or men who claimed to be under his command but were actually little more than freelance vigilantes. Indeed, one of these, Shubal Merritt, a former soldier in the revolutionary army who had argued with his commanding officer and switched sides in the war, was notorious for killing and robbing throughout Westchester County, supposedly on behalf of the British, before being shot in a tavern brawl in New Rochelle in 1783. Yet, Shubal was widely hailed as a hero by loyalist residents of the county despite his reputation for horrible atrocities.

Skinners and Other Dubious Patriots

The Americans had their own irregulars in the neutral zone. Associated loosely, if at all, with local militia units, these men— some of them called the Westchester Guides—served as spies, guides and assassins of loyalist neighbors or suspected English patrols living in or moving through this dangerous area. When loyalist residents were expelled wholesale by the American authorities from towns like Peekskill and had to make their way through the neutral ground to the safety of English-held White Plains, they were easy prey for the Westchester Guides and similar groups who lay in wait in the heavily wooded forests along the road southward to rob and even kill them. Whether such men were motivated by patriotism for the cause of independence or were merely opportunists driven by greed has long been a subject of disagreement. Perhaps, in many instances the two motives combined to produce a deadly result for many of the loyalist residents in the region.

The most notorious of these American guerrilla bands was the so-called Skinners, active mostly in and around Tarrytown. Their name came from the fact that they literally skinned or stole from the loyalists—or simply victimized any person they chose, regardless of political loyalties. They were, for the most part, lawless freebooters, sometimes aided and abetted by soldiers in the regular colonial militia. Often they went beyond looting and burning to commit atrocities such as hanging their victims by the thumbs, cutting off their fingers, suspending them in sacks of water, covering their bodies with burning coals and even killing them—all because these unfortunates were supposedly loyal to the British cause.

Homes and properties, abandoned out of fear by the fleeing loyalists, were immediately seized by the civil and military authorities and turned over to the army or to loyal Americans for use in the military effort or as payment for services rendered to the rebel cause. The threat of all this activity to the British cause was well understood in that camp. Such ruthless treatment of their many sympathizers in the region—at least half of the population—could only weaken internal resistance to the revolutionary cause by discouraging pro-British attitudes and by assuring more food and supplies for the beleaguered colonial army. On numerous occasions, troops were sent northward into the neutral ground to try to clear the area of such marauders as the Westchester Guards and the Skinners and to give comfort to the loyalist residents thereby securing their homes and farms and occasionally retaking entire towns from the Americans. But in the end, the English never succeeded in pacifying the region and it remained a dangerous no man's land for most of the war.

As early as the fall of 1777, the neutral ground was so devastated by actions of these bands of robbers and killers that the Reverend Timothy Dwight, chaplain to General Samuel Parson's Connecticut Brigade stationed at the time at West Point, wrote that the residents of the area

> feared everybody who they saw, and loved nobody....Their houses were in a great measure scenes of desolation. Their furniture was extensively plundered or broken into pieces. The walls, floors and windows were injured by violence and decay....Their cattle were gone. Their enclosures were burnt down where they were capable of becoming fuel, and in many cases thrown down where they were not. Their fields were covered with rank growth and wild grass. Amid all this appearance of desolation, nothing struck my own eye more forcibly than the sight of this great road, the passage from New York to Boston. Where I had heretofore seen a continual succession of horses and carriages, and life and bustle lend sprightliness to all the environing objects, not a single solitary traveler was visible from week to week, or from month to month.[9]

---

[9] Ward, op. cit, 19.

In his novel, *The Old Continental and the Price of Liberty,* set in the neutral ground, James Kirke Paulding puts the following words of desperation in the mouth of a local farm woman:

I have no friends. I am a poor lone woman and, friend or foe, everyone plunders and insults me. The Cowboys come here as friends and steal my fowls; the Skinners say they are my friends and drive away cattle; the Redcoats and Yagers [Hessian mercenaries] are plundering everything they can lay their hands on, break everything they cannot carry away and then go away cursing me as a rebel. But God's will be done; only don't murder me, gentlemen![10]

The plight of James Paulding's fictional character may well have been based on the real-life experience of his cousin, John's mother, Sarah. While the men in her family were off fighting in the war, Sarah was alone at home one day when their farm was plundered by a Cowboy raiding party. Sarah was assaulted and perhaps raped. The record reports, vaguely, that she was "compelled to submit to indignities."[11]

A full and dramatic depiction of life in the neutral ground is James Fennimore Cooper's classic, *The Spy: A Tale of the Neutral Ground,* the second novel by the famed American writer, published in 1821 less than forty years after the Revolution. Cooper lived in Westchester County while writing the novel and drew it from first-hand accounts of natives of the region. The Cowboys and Skinners spring to life in the pages of his book, as Cooper weaves a tale of conflict, intrigue, romance, patriotism, betrayal and tragedy with families divided from one another and within themselves over the issue of national independence. The hero of Cooper's novel is Harvey Birch, a spy for the Americans under the direct command of General Washington. Birch poses as an English spy so that he can bring back vital information to the American commander. There are several references in the novel to a real spy story—the most notorious in American history—that had occurred in this same neutral zone just two decades earlier.

[10] James Paulding, *The Old Continental and the Price of Liberty,* 1846, 90.
[11] Larry Reynolds, *James Kirke Paulding 1778-1860,* Boston, 1984, 2.

John Paulding as a young man
*Courtesy of Branch Libraries, The New York Public Library,
Astor, Lenox and Tilden Foundations*

— CHAPTER 3 —

John the Patriot

John Paulding, known to history as "Patriot John," was destined to become the most famous and celebrated of the residents of the neutral ground. He was descended from a long line of Pauldings who had arrived from Holland in the late seventeenth century and been living in the Hudson River Valley ever since. He was a poor relation of the famous aforementioned William Paulding of Tarrytown and the older cousin of one of America's first accomplished writers, James Kirke Paulding.

A Boyhood in the Neutral Ground

John was born on a farm just east of Tarrytown, New York, in an area variously known as East View, East Tarrytown and, later, the Paulding Farmstead. The Paulding house had been built (or rebuilt from an older structure) by Joseph Paulding in about 1753. Joseph, who had never been able to match the commercial successes of his siblings, had brought his wife, Susannah White Paulding, and three sons, Joseph III, William and Peter out of New York City to live in this less expensive rural environment. A year later, a fourth son, John, was born. In 1757, eldest son, Joseph, brought his new bride, Sarah Gardiner, into the little house and a year after that, on October 16, 1758, their son, John, was born. Crammed into a small rundown house with baby John were his grandmother and grandfather, "an aged couple whose snow-white locks and stooping figures bore testimony to a long pilgrimage through this vale of tears,"[12] his mother and father and his three uncles.

---

[12] James Paulding, op. cit., 5.

The farmhouse where young John Paulding grew to manhood was an ancient pile, bearing the date 1688. The small stone structure, in an advanced state of decay, supported a roof heavily laden with decaying moss—a far cry from the elegant riverside mansion and city townhouse of John's uncle William and baby cousin James Kirke. There was a bucolic charm to this wooded and pastoral terrain that characterized the living environment of most Americans in the mid-eighteenth century. When John stepped out of his house in the morning he did not see crowded commercial streets or a busy harbor filled with merchant ships. His view from the hill on which his house stood was of a small stream meandering through native trees and between small mountains that flanked acres of green meadow stretching out before him. Behind the house was an ample pond supplying both water and fish for the family.

John Paulding enjoyed few boyhood luxuries. He experienced the frequent privations born of dependence on the vagaries of nature and the family's health and energy. His own character would be typical of those formed by American rural life at that time, comprising traits which many from Thomas Jefferson onward, including writers, James Fennimore Cooper and James Kirke Paulding, have seen as characteristic of the defining values in American history: lack of sophistication (and pride in it), rugged individualism, self-reliance and suspicion of authority whether governmental, religious or commercial.

An Intrepid Youth

By the time war broke out, John's grandfather had died (in 1773) and his father soon left home to fight with Captain George Comb's company in the militia. His three uncles were away much of the time serving in various units of the Revolutionary army and militia. John was usually left at home alone to tend the farm and look after his mother and aged grandmother. Although the three may have stayed for extended periods far behind American lines in Putnam County with their more affluent relatives, they were usually at home in the dangerous neutral ground, surviving as best they could in this increasingly desolate and dangerous no man's land.

The nineteen-year-old John was itching to get into the fight. From time to time he would leave the farm and join a local militia unit or a volunteer group that was assisting the militia in some particular assignment, usually involving attacking loyalist Cowboy bands that were roving the countryside terrorizing residents and extorting crops and livestock from uncooperative patriot farmers like himself. After one such engagement, John received a commendation from Colonel Philip Van Courtland, the militia commander in Peekskill.

By one account, John, at about age twenty and stretching to the atypical height of well over six feet, was "a superb specimen of manhood" who was "handsome, active and possessed an intrepidy as well as a cool self-possession in time of danger."[13] His reputation as a daring and courageous patriot began to grow in the Hudson Valley region after a dramatic event at his farm in 1779. At the time, John, like his father, was a member of the Westchester militia under command of a Captain Requa. He was on leave, as was his brother William, so that the two men could do some necessary work in the fields. While at work, they were attacked by a gang of five Cowboys they had caught trying to steal their horses. The raiders captured John and William and were about to lead them off along with the horses when John grabbed for his musket and managed to get off a shot.

The startled Cowboys fled across the fields with the Paulding brothers and their aroused neighbors in pursuit all the way to the outskirts of White Plains. Satisfied that they had driven off the bandits, John and his companions were on their way back to Tarrytown when, unluckily, a troop of English soldiers surprised them and took them prisoner. This time there was no escape. John and several others were taken all the way to New York City and imprisoned in Bayard's Sugar Mill on Wall Street, known as the "Old Sugar House Prison," the most notorious of the British military prisons.

The prison house itself was a huge structure of red stone with narrow grated windows, located in the northeast corner of the Old Dutch Church yard that was being used by the occupying British as a riding school. Prisoners were confined "in separate cellars,

---

[13] Patterson, op. cit., 137; James Paulding, op. cit., 6.

little better than dungeons" with no flooring and garbage strewn underfoot. The overall environment was one of "utter neglect and desolation…where nothing but a dim twilight reigned all day and nothing could be seen but the gravestones in the churchyard."[14]

According to Alexander Boyce, a Tarrytown neighbor and fellow prisoner with John in the Sugar House, conditions were appalling. "The prisoners were thrown together…without any order, and without the least care for their health or ordinary comfort. We believed that the English were constantly trying to poison us. We very often found broken glass in our bread and pepper." Boyce reports that the daily food allowance was scanty, consisting of two ounces of meat and eight ounces of bread. There were no fireplaces. A few sticks of wood were handed out each day for building a cooking fire on the floor of the cell. As there was no ventilation, the smoke from these fires was nearly suffocating.[15]

Despite the seemingly impossible odds, the irrepressible John Paulding soon found an opportunity to escape. There is no way to improve upon the words of Alexander Boyce as he describes his friend's dramatic escape in a letter written less than two decades after the event:

> I was a prisoner with John Paulding in the Old Sugar House. We were sometimes allowed to walk into the yard. When we came into the yard from the Sugar House, we were counted and again when we returned. Around the Sugar House was a picket fence about as high as a man's face (five feet). The English were building a new picket fence a great deal higher than the old one and had nearly completed it when, one evening, the prisoners were let into the yard as usual. The sun was about an hour high. John Paulding was near me and leaned against the picket near a space where the old fence was taken down and the new one [was] not yet completed. The sentry was stationed on the outside of the fence and passed the open space as he walked

---

[14] James Paulding, op. cit., 119-120.

[15] Taken from a letter to John Paulding's son, Hiram Paulding, from Alexander Boyce written in 1818, shortly after John's death, in Rebecca Paulding Meade, *The Life of Hiram Paulding*, New York, 1910, 275.

to and fro. Paulding, who was watching for an opportunity, walked out of the prison yard as the sentry's back was turned toward him, and deliberately continued up the street without being noticed or particularly remarked by anyone. He continued on in this way until we lost sight of him, and no one except the prisoners had any suspicion that he was [not] one of the British soldiers, as he wore at the time a refugee's coat that he received in exchange for his own.[16]

Although Boyce does not report where Paulding came by his Hessian coat, we know that it was given to him by a friend named Nathan Levinus who owned a stable near the prison and helped him secure a boat to cross the river into New Jersey under cover of darkness. Meantime, Boyce tells us, Paulding's absence was discovered at the prison and "search was made for him in every direction, but without getting any trace of him." Stopping at a small house for a brief rest the next day, Paulding cleverly inquired which was the road going *to* New York for fear the woman, who might well have been a loyalist, would suspect that he was not one himself but a rebel traveling *from* the city.

Once back in the Hudson highlands, Paulding was stopped by an American patrol which, understandably, took him to be a loyalist spy and carried him off to be questioned by the Marquis de Lafayette who was nearby at Weehawken. Visiting Lafayette at the time, fortunately for Paulding, was Colonel Van Courtland from Peekskill who informed Lafayette of Paulding's patriotic exploits in the neutral zone and arranged for his release, with thanks, to rejoin his unit.[17]

Reports of such exploits by John Paulding quickly spread throughout the region making him a local hero of sorts. Soon, on September 23, 1780, he would keep his appointment with destiny and step onto the stage of national history, along with two other much better known men. Before long he would come to exemplify the American prototype of the common man as hero: the sturdy yeoman of the new nation, the backbone of the new democracy. In future years, many would know him, simply, as "Patriot John."

---

[16] Ibid.
[17] Ibid.

Le Général ARNOLD

déserté de l'Armée des Etats-Unis

le 3 Octobre 1780.

Benedict Arnold at time of treason, drawn by du Simitier
Courtesy of the New-York Historical Society

— C H A P T E R 4 —

Benedict the Traitor

The second of the three men whose lives intersected on September 23, 1780, in such a way as to change forever the course of American history is far better known than John Paulding. His name, in fact, is virtually a household term throughout the world and universally synonymous with "traitor."

Despite the worthy effort of some historians to recast Benedict Arnold as a misunderstood hero, most Americans continue to regard him as the worst villain in history, the secular Judas Iscariot of the national drama. He is held in such low regard because he almost cost the United States its birth as an independent nation.[18]

The Rearing of a Traitor

How did this once-courageous American patriot become a traitor? Was there something in his character or background that disposed him to sell out his country after he had been one of her most daring and courageous defenders? Was he so unfairly and unjustly treated by his countrymen that, out of bitterness, he could not reasonably be expected to resist the temptation to seek his fortune in the tents of his country's mortal enemy? Was he simply a greedy, self-interested egomaniac who regarded himself as above allegiance to his country? To attempt an answer to this question— one that still stirs controversy among historians—and to discover what brought Benedict Arnold to that fateful September day in 1780, we turn back the clock nearly forty years to the beginnings of Arnold's life in colonial New England.

---

[18] For a recent favorable treatment of Arnold, see James Martin, *Benedict Arnold Revolutionary Hero*. New York, 1997.

Born in January 1741 in Norwich Town, Connecticut, Benedict was a fifth generation New Englander, almost as purely American as it was possible to be. His original American ancestor had been with Roger Williams in the founding of Rhode Island (the Providence Plantations) in 1636, and his great grandfather, whose Christian name he bore, had been the governor of that colony. His own father, another Benedict, was a prominent merchant who married well, amassed a large fleet of ships and prospered in international trade. Unfortunately for young Benedict, by the time he was entering his teens his father had become a serious alcoholic and managed to lose most of the family fortune in a series of disastrous business deals.[19]

Perhaps because he lacked adequate parental supervision, Benedict became something of a young hooligan. Stories are told of his boyhood pranks, ranging from spreading out glass along foot paths so that small children would cut their feet, to robbing bird's nests and starting fires. Surely as all mothers of difficult children, Hannah Arnold tried her best to turn her son around. She scraped together what money she could and sent her eleven-year-old son off to boarding school to learn discipline as well as his ABCs. There, Benedict had an excellent teacher who taught him some Latin, French and basic math. Just as the precocious youth was settling in nicely to his studies, his father's drinking finally exhausted the family resources and his mother had to withdraw him from school. Before long the boy, now thirteen, was running wild along the Norwich waterfront, boarding ships, climbing and jumping from masts and generally making a dangerous nuisance of himself.

This time his distraught mother sent him off to live and work as an apprentice in the business of one of the leading families of the town, her prosperous relatives, the Lathrops. Brothers Daniel and Joshua Lathrop owned and operated what today would be

---

[19] A reliable and balanced biography of Arnold is William Stone, *Benedict Arnold Patriot and Traitor*, New York, 1990. Still of value is the Jared Sparks classic, *The Life and Treason of Benedict Arnold*, Boston, 1835. Also useful are Willard Wallace, *Traitorous Hero: The Life and Fortunes of Benedict Arnold*, New York, 1954, and Wilson Barry, *Benedict Arnold a Traitor in Our Midst*, Montreal, 2001.

understood as the largest "department store" in Norwich from which they sold an impressive array of drugs, wines, food products and manufactured goods from England and the West Indies. Here young Benedict worked as an apprentice while living nearby in the Lathrop mansion where his surrogate mother, Daniel Lathrop's wife, Jerusha, raised him as a son, providing for his continuing education, including instruction in the manners and graces of their social class.

Benedict was restless under this benevolent but restrictive regimen. No doubt he resented living as a virtual servant in the home of a relative who had prospered while his own profligate father had squandered his future on alcohol, left his mother nearly destitute and himself without good prospects. In 1758, after three years with the Lathrops, the seventeen-year-old had had enough. He wanted his freedom and some adventure as well. He would make his own way in the world. Just west of Connecticut, in Westchester County, New York, opportunity beckoned.

Acquiring the Taste of Adventure

Captain Reuben Lockwood was accepting young men like Benedict into his company of New York troopers that was a part of the British force fighting the French in that colony. The nearly century-long contest between Europe's two dominant powers was in its last years when it spilled over onto the North American continent into a war for hegemony on this side of the Atlantic, especially for control of the great river basins and watersheds of the Hudson, the St. Lawrence and Ohio Rivers and for the important cities and trading centers lying within reach of those vital waterways. This episode in the larger European contest has been dubbed by American historians, the French and Indian War.

In the portion of New York's upper Hudson Valley where Captain Lockwood's troop operated, the key military objectives of the British were to gain control of Fort Ticonderoga and Lake Champlain and the water and land routes that led northward to Quebec City, Montreal and the St. Lawrence River. The French controlled most of this region; they enjoyed lucrative fur trading with the local Native American tribes. The British, under the revitalized ministry of William Pitt the Elder, viewed French dominance in Canada, upper New York state and Vermont as a serious threat to their American empire to the south and were determined to drive them out of the area altogether and claim these northern lands for themselves.

In the ensuing battles, the local tribes were encouraged by both the British and French to raid, plunder and kill military and civilian personnel in and near one another's encampments and to terrorize local inhabitants into supporting one side or the other. It was a vicious little war in which feelings ran so high on both sides that some of the participants who were to play leading roles in the War for Independence just a few years later, including George Washington, could earn their military spurs fighting with British units. Others, including Benedict Arnold, were to develop a visceral hatred for the French that endured for the rest of their lives.

As young Benedict slipped undetected out of his aunt's house in Norwich in 1757 and walked the whole way westward to join Captain Lockwood's English troops in Westchester County, he could have had little inkling of what in later years would await him in most of those regions then contested by the French and British. The youth saw no military action and within a year he was discovered as a runaway and forced to return to Norwich. But by this time he had caught a fever—and fervor—for military life of which he would never be cured. Clearly, here was his route to independence, fame and fortune. Before long, he had successfully badgered his mother into letting him return to Captain Lockwood's unit, and within a year he was back in uniform as a member of the New York militia.

This time, Benedict stayed for only a few months. When he learned that his mother was seriously ill, he deserted and hurried home to be with her. A forty shilling reward was offered for the capture and return of the young fugitive. Hannah was indeed terminally ill. She hid her prodigal son in her house and later sent him to hide in the homes of some friends when the British came looking for him. She was dead within a year, and the deeply grieved Benedict Arnold returned to the New York militia in Westchester County, this time to serve in a different unit. There is no record of any action being taken against him for his desertion.

With the war against the French effectively over after the British victory on the Plains of Abraham in 1759, Benedict returned to Norwich and entered his uncle's business as an agent sailing in the Lathrop merchant ships trading in the West Indies and England. He quickly caught the bug for the life of a merchant trader, reveling in the risky high stakes of making unsecured business deals at dockside and carousing in West Indian ports with good wine and available women.

The year 1762 was an eventful one in the twenty-seven-year-old Benedict's life. His alcoholic father finally died. His wealthy uncle and patron, Daniel Lathrop, paid off his brother-in-law's considerable debts, gave a £500 gift to his nephew—a small fortune at the time—and made him a "trainee" in his Caribbean trading business with obvious promise of a bright future with the company. Benedict gladly accepted the generous gift and the freedom from his father's debts but declined service with his uncle. Instead, he took his new-found wealth, including money from the sale of his father's house, and the experience he had gained on Lathrop's ships, and left Norwich altogether to set up his own trading company, complete with apothecary shop, some sixty miles to the east in New Haven on Long Island Sound. Lathrop's support was unfailing as he financed his nephew's trip to London to purchase goods for his new shop.

Once in London, Arnold bought huge supplies of drugs, tea, books, paints, maps, pictures, jewelry and other goods for his new shop—mostly on credit. Then he sailed to the West Indies and added to his inventory with rum, more drugs, jewelry and other goods, again mostly purchased on credit. He thoroughly enjoyed the adventurous life of a merchant trader, exuding a charm and self-confidence that drew women to him and led him into frequent confrontations with other adventurers. He became involved for a time in the potentially lucrative and illegal molasses trade that involved shipping molasses, rum and sugar from the West Indies in exchange for lumber, livestock and food—all without payment of taxes, especially the high tax on molasses.

Off to a Bad Start

During these years Benedict Arnold came into contact with some of the more nefarious seaman of the day. According to some reports, he displayed the arrogant and highly egocentric attitudes of a bully who would brook no opposition to his words or deeds and was quick to perceive insults in any comment that did not support him. More than once, he provoked duels with rival ship captains and merchants he claimed had insulted him. He was an excellent shot and superb swordsman. Invariably he would wound his opponents and then demand an apology. Before long, he was disliked if not despised by many men who knew him, although women apparently admired and often adored him. On one occasion, his beloved sister, named Hannah like their mother, fell in love with a Frenchman. Arnold, who hated the French, forbade her to see him, but she persisted until Arnold caught the two together. He pulled out his revolver and shot at the Frenchman who fled, never to return.

Before long Arnold was deeply in debt, mostly to London merchants. His business was in ruins. He needed a new outlet for his energies. The growing sentiment for revolution against Britain was perfectly timed as an acceptable outlet for his often violent machismo. In 1765 he joined the Sons of Liberty which had been organized to resist the Stamp Act and other levies on trade. In Connecticut alone over 1,000 men joined this revolutionary group. Soon Arnold was a leading local firebrand, writing articles against the English and leading open rebellions against British officials in New Haven.

The colony was deeply divided on the issue of separation from England. There were two anti-revolution groups in New Haven, consisting mostly of leading merchants and landowners. On one side were the Old Lights of the First Ecclesiastical Society and leading members of Trinity Episcopal Church. Opposing these conservatives were the so-called Radicals who were drawn largely from the New Lights in the non-Episcopal churches, lesser merchants and the faculty at Yale. Arnold was a leader of this latter group and was soon organizing a company of militia to follow him into battle.

Even as he was becoming prominent in the radical revolutionary movement in 1765, Arnold continued to ply his failing career as a merchant, displaying the violent temper that had marred his youth and would continue to characterize his life and career as an adult. In 1766 one Peter Bowles, a sailor on one of his trading ships, claimed that he had not been paid what was owed him for services at sea. When Arnold refused to pay, Bowles turned his employer in to the New Haven authorities for non-payment of the debt and, while he was at it, offered proof that Arnold had engaged in smuggling and had not paid duties owed on his cargoes. No one doubted this as it was the custom among most merchant traders to smuggle goods in order to avoid payment of taxes to the British. In retaliation, Arnold and his gang beat Bowles publicly in the town square and drove the hapless sailor out of town. A grand jury was convened to make an example of Arnold and his radical thugs. At trial he was found guilty and required to pay a fine of fifty shillings.

During the years just before the Revolution Arnold owned three ships, *Fortune*, *Sally* and *Three Brothers*. These carried his cargoes of horses, pork and lumber to the West Indies and brought back rum and molasses. He also traded in Quebec where he bought most of the horses that he traded in the West Indies. In New Haven he built himself a large mansion on three acres along the waterfront, complete with carriage house, wharfs, fruit trees and a picket fence. He completed his climb to social prominence by marrying into one of New Haven's wealthiest families, the Mansfields. Margaret was a shy young woman of twenty-two when the twenty-five-year-old Arnold married her in 1767. At first he was passionately in love. Although they had three sons, their relationship soon soured. Margaret was almost pathologically withdrawn and moody, not at all a good match for her exuberant and ambitious husband.

Before long, rumors were spreading in New Haven about Arnold's affairs with married women while he was in the West Indies and his subsequent duels with their cuckolded mates. Some, though probably not all, of these rumors were unfounded. What is undoubtedly true is that those who knew Arnold increasingly regarded him as a violent, self-aggrandizing and ruthless person. Despite his philandering, he apparently still loved his wife and was deeply hurt when she refused for some time to go near him. He also bitterly resented the damage done to his social reputation by those who carried these stories home from the Indies.

Becoming a Hero

By the early 1770s, Arnold had found some escape from his marital, financial and social problems through increasing involvement in the revolutionary activities of the Sons of Liberty. Connecticut was so divided on the issue of separation that few prominent people could be found to represent the colony at the first meeting of the Continental Congress in 1774 in Philadelphia. Arnold was more than willing to serve. The Connecticut delegation, including Arnold, was hosted while in Philadelphia by Judge Edward Shippen, a leading figure in the city. Here it was that Arnold first met Peggy Shippen, then only fourteen but already a beauty known for her flirtatiousness. What the two thought of each other at this first meeting we can only guess. No doubt, Peggy enjoyed the challenge of beguiling her father's guests from Connecticut, including the already notorious adventurer Benedict Arnold. Just as surely, Arnold would have been captivated by the young beauty. Certainly neither could guess the future they would soon share—and help to shape.

While Arnold was in Philadelphia tending to business and to Peggy, his Sons of Liberty back in New Haven were busy wreaking havoc on British installations and conducting violent terrorist-like attacks on the persons and property of some of the leading British sympathizers. Before long, the Sons of Liberty were the dominant military force in Connecticut. Ignoring a decision by the government in New Haven to stay out of the conflict brewing at Lexington and Concord in neighboring Massachusetts in April of 1775, Arnold led a contingent of about fifty volunteers from the New Haven village green to Boston. The great cleric, Jonathan Edwards, later known as the founder of American Transcendentalism, blessed the group as it gathered on the green, with Arnold standing in front of his men bedecked in a brilliant uniform of red jacket, white breeches and silver buttons.

Once in Massachusetts, Arnold presented a plan to the colony's Committee of Safety for the capture of the British garrison at Fort Ticonderoga on Lake Champlain in northeastern New York. He was forthwith awarded a commission as colonel in the Massachusetts militia with permission to recruit a force of 400 men. He was also given a supply of guns and ammunition and £100 for other supplies. Resplendent in his showy uniform and filled with prospects for the fame that surely awaited him as a hero of the fledgling American Revolution, Arnold set forth to the northeast through Vermont and New Hampshire to Lake Champlain.

Unfortunately for his hopes of fame and glory, Arnold's home state of Connecticut, at about the same time, commissioned Vermonter Ethan Allen to perform the same task. This circumstance produced a race between these two vainglorious men to be the first to reach Fort Ticonderoga. Once there, they argued at length about who would command the attack. In the event, it was Allen who took command and got most of the credit for the capture of the fort, leaving Arnold jealous and embittered. Nevertheless, immediately after their victory in May of 1775, the two rivals jointly planned a follow-up campaign to march northward into Canada and fight the British in Quebec. But the Continental Congress vetoed any attack on Canada and even decided to abandon the recently captured Fort Ticonderoga. Once again feeling betrayed by those in authority over him, Arnold quit his military command altogether in June and headed home for New Haven. En route, he received even worse news. His wife, Margaret, only thirty years old, had just died leaving him a widower with two small children in his charge—seven-year-old Benedict IV and six-year-old Richard. Fortunately, his devoted sister, Hannah, was willing to move into his splendid house and raise his children for him.

A few months later, Arnold was back in the fray, accepting a difficult commission from Congress to march northward with a large force and join General Richard Montgomery in attacking Quebec. Montgomery, a former officer in the British army, had captured St. John's and Montreal in November and was now poised to attack Quebec from inside Canada once Arnold's force arrived to cut off a British retreat to New England. In September, Arnold left with a force of about 1,100 men, including ten companies from New England, two from Pennsylvania and one from Virginia, along with a naval contingent of eleven ships.

It was a horrendous march northward over four hundred miles of torturous New England winter terrain, through alternately frozen and muddy forests, across swollen and often icy rivers, streams and lakes. In one of the most difficult and heroic marches in all of U.S. military history, hundreds of the men froze to death or died of starvation. Finally, in November, after some forty-five days, Arnold arrived at the walls of Quebec City with fewer than 600 half-starved men. He immediately laid siege to the city while waiting for the arrival of Montgomery from Montreal.

Through a combination of poor communication and unfortunate caution on the part of both Montgomery and Arnold, the joint attack did not occur until early December by which time the British had reinforced their garrison and now greatly outnumbered the Americans. On December 30, Arnold attacked. His forces scaled the walls and fought in hand-to-hand street-by-street combat; Arnold stayed at the head of his men urging them on with the example of his own remarkable courage under fire. Despite a serious wound in his left leg, which left him permanently crippled, Arnold fought on bravely. After a few days, his outnumbered force was pushed back out of the city. The invasion had failed. After a few months of maintaining a siege outside the wall, the American force retreated to Montreal.

Arnold was the last to leave the scene of battle at Quebec, dramatically shooting his own horse as he climbed into a canoe so that the enemy could not have use of it. Despite the failure at Quebec, Arnold, who had shown incredible personal courage throughout the campaign and had come to be loved by his troops, was hailed as a national hero. Washington praised him publicly and had the U.S. Congress promote him to the rank of brigadier general. Arnold had finally found his niche in life, that place where his apparently insatiable need for respect, greatness and wealth might one day be satisfied.

A Checkered Career

Arnold's attitude during his subsequent military career oscillated between fits of rage, petulance and disappointment over what he regarded as inadequate recognition for his achievements and overt demonstrations of his lack of judgment and unfettered greed and ambition. To be sure, his military accomplishments were usually noteworthy and often extraordinary; but his behavior following the battlefield successes was just as often reprehensible.

During the occupation at Montreal, following the retreat from Quebec City, he sought and received permission from Congress to commandeer food and clothing from Canadian civilians for his starving and bedraggled troops. Going far beyond his authorization, he oversaw mass looting and pillaging by his men, who behaved more like a terrorist rabble than an army. For this breach of orders Arnold was court-martialed, probably unfairly given the severe circumstances he faced in Montreal. Although he was subsequently acquitted when General Gates turned the case over to Congress, Arnold displayed such egotism, intemperance and anger toward those who accused and judged him that nearly everyone involved developed a strong dislike for him. He seemed totally lacking in tact, much less the political savvy needed to climb the ladder of promotion in the military. His reputation was thereafter severely tarnished with the very men who would determine his future.

Between the autumn of 1776 and spring of 1777 Arnold was involved in a number of military actions. He displayed remarkable ingenuity and bravery in his command on Lake Champlain in September and October where he had to build a fleet of warships from scratch, using local green timber. His assignment was to defend the lake from a large invading British naval force led by the *Inflexible* with eighteen twelve-pound cannon, the *Maria* and the *Carleton* with fourteen and twelve six-pounders respectively and the *Thunderer* that mounted twenty four-pounders. His own rag-tag fleet of much smaller ships included one vessel with eighteen-pound cannon but the others mounted only four- and six-pounders.

On October 11, Sir Guy Carleton led his fleet, carrying a large contingent of British troops along with some 1,000 Native American warriors on board southward up the lake. Although ultimately defeated and forced to retreat to Crown Point, Arnold displayed brilliant strategy and great personal courage under fire as his ships wreaked havoc on Carleton's great fleet, even while suffering high casualties in sunken ships and lost men. In the aftermath, Carleton, badly scarred by the encounter, withdrew from the lake and returned to Canada without retaking Fort Ticonderoga.

Once again, Arnold, in apparent defeat, was rightly hailed a hero. By inflicting damage on Carleton and showing incredible determination when outnumbered, he discouraged the English commander from pressing his advantage and moving on down the Hudson to New York City. To Arnold's horror, however, his heroism was not rewarded by the promotion to major general that he so much coveted. Instead, he was passed over as Congress promoted five decidedly inferior officers to this rank. Clearly, his attitudes had offended his civilian superiors and they were expressing their personal dislike of him, hero or no. Arnold was incensed and at once offered his resignation to Washington.

His troubles were magnified in May when Colonel John Brown petitioned Congress to court-martial or at least reprimand him for what Brown claimed were numerous instances of corruption and malfeasance in the conduct of his duties. The two men had clashed at the very beginning of their military careers during early battles in Vermont and at Fort Ticonderoga. Congress ultimately rejected Brown's petition possibly because the colonel appeared to them to be as arrogant and self-serving as the general. No matter who was at fault, the entire affair left one more blemish on Arnold's reputation with Congress and many of his fellow officers.

In July, Arnold resigned his commission. He did so in a pique over Congress's failure to reimburse him for what he felt were legitimate personal expenses incurred during recent battles in Connecticut. Washington wrote a letter to Congress commending Arnold and requesting that Congress simply ignore his letter of resignation, which they did. But Arnold's action was yet another reason for Congress to resent what many regarded as his grasping and self-aggrandizing behavior.

Arnold's courage was on display again just a few months later in Connecticut when, at the battle of Ridgefield Court in April of 1777, he led his troops, outnumbered four-to-one, in hand-to-hand combat. Again he was defeated, but not before his horse had been struck with some nine bullets. As he lay on the battlefield with his foot caught in the dead horse's stirrup, a British soldier raced toward him ordering him to surrender. "Not yet," screamed Arnold as he coolly shot the soldier dead before scampering to his feet and racing to safety with a hail of bullets chasing him. The very next day, he was back in battle at a skirmish in Campo where he harassed and delayed the advancing British governor and general, Sir William Tryon.

Within weeks, Arnold's heroism under fire was hailed even by those who disliked him personally. With Washington's enthusiastic endorsement, he was promoted by Congress to the rank of major general in June of 1777. A few months later he would reach the highest point of his achievement and fame as a hero of the American Revolution at the battles of Fort Stanwix along the Mohawk River just west of the Hudson and at Freeman's Farm and Bemis Heights just north of Albany—victories that led to Burgoyne's historic surrender at Saratoga on October 17, 1777.

At Fort Stanwix, Arnold once again displayed his courage and ingenuity by convincing local Native Americans that they should abandon their British alliances and join him; indeed they already regarded him as one of the greatest warriors among the warring white men. When Arnold relieved the British siege of the fort and entered it on August 23, he was hailed as a conquering hero. Arnold's successes did not sit well with his superior officer, General Horatio Gates, who had taken command of the northern army in July. Gates regarded Arnold as an unreliable and disobedient officer who sought his own glory rather than the success of the overall war effort. The two men were to clash soon again at the decisive battles near Saratoga.

Meanwhile, General Howe, who Burgoyne assumed was moving up the Hudson to meet him and complete the conquest of New England and New York, had a plan of his own that did not include aiding Burgoyne. He claimed to have different orders supporting his own plan, which was to recapture Philadelphia. In the event, Burgoyne was never effectively supported from the south. True enough, Howe was relieved of his command by Sir Henry Clinton in May, and, after much delay, Clinton moved up the Hudson in early October, capturing some forts along the way. He was too late to be any help to Burgoyne who by this time was engaged in deadly and decisive combat with the Americans just north of Albany.

On September 19, a fateful battle of the Revolution took place at Freeman's Farm. Gates and Burgoyne faced off in one of the bloodiest encounters of the war. Once again, Arnold was the hero of the day, displaying his usual aggressive courage under fire, refusing to give up the attack despite repeated failures to take the British position, urging his men on in assault after assault. While not providing victory for the Americans, Arnold and his men inflicted such casualties and displayed such determination that Burgoyne withdrew from the field. Gates made the mistake of ordering Arnold not to pursue Burgoyne, thereby assuring that the British general would have sufficient forces to fight another day. In his report to General Washington and Congress on the battle at Freeman's Farm, the vindictive Gates failed to mention Arnold's pivotal role in driving Burgoyne from the field. In fact, he went out of his way to demean his courageous subordinate and went so far as to relieve Arnold of all command.

Less than three weeks later on October 7, Arnold disobeyed orders and took over command of American forces in the midst of the battle at nearby Bemis Heights, a battle that many historians regard as the turning point in the war. Racing onto the field at a critical point in the battle, the unfairly dismissed Arnold, who had no business even being there, galloped to the head of the troops shouting, "Follow me!" In the style of the World War II general George Patton Arnold rallied the men and spurred them on to victory. The Americans followed their beloved leader, attacking again and again and suffering huge casualties before finally surrounding the enemy in a brilliant maneuver orchestrated by Arnold. It was all the stuff of legend. Like Patton after him, Arnold was regarded by his superiors as a maverick and resented for his ability to gain his men's respect and loyalty.

In the final assault at Bemis Heights, the fearless Arnold was shot in the same leg that had been wounded at Quebec. As for Burgoyne, he retreated a short distance up the river to Saratoga where he surrendered his entire force of nearly 6,000 men to Gates on October 16. Clinton then retreated all the way down the Hudson to White Plains, abandoning the forts he had recently captured, consolidating British forces in New York and conceding all of New England, New York and much of New Jersey and Pennsylvania to the rebels. The French, observing all of this retreating by the British, finally decided officially to enter the war on behalf of the Americans.

Surely, if any man deserved to be hailed as the hero of the day it was Benedict Arnold. He was briefly acclaimed as such, especially when he returned to his native Connecticut in the spring of 1778 after a long and difficult treatment and convalescence for his painful and debilitating leg wound. Congress restored him to his earlier rank of brigadier general, but his wounds prevented him from taking another field command. In June, Washington appointed him military commander of Philadelphia, just a day after General Clinton had left the city. It was a nearly impossible job, however, for which Arnold was especially ill-suited.

The Philadelphia Command

The major problem in governing Philadelphia was that it had always been deeply divided between British loyalists and American revolutionaries. Much of the most valuable real and personal property in the city belonged to loyalists who had prospered during the British occupation and now were fearful of losing their wealth as patriots moved in to confiscate assets they felt had been held by traitors. As commander of the city, Arnold responded by immediately declaring martial law, closing all shops and confiscating for military use all imported goods from Europe and the Indies. (Presumably these were ordered by the retreating British and their loyalist friends remaining in the city). A huge public uproar followed this proclamation. Even though the shop closings lasted only a week, resentment remained about what was regarded as arbitrary action by the new military commander. This anger increased when Arnold proceeded to live extravagantly, traveling about the city in high style, entertaining lavishly in his large mansion on his ninety-six-acre estate in Fairmont Park. At the same time, he was engaging in a number of apparently illegal business dealings that involved use of his authority as commander to benefit himself personally.

Before long the 5'7" black-haired, green-eyed, badly crippled thirty-eight year-old Benedict Arnold, hobbling about with an elaborately jeweled cane and exhibiting an uncommon self-confidence, was courting the lovely Peggy Shippen. The first time the two had met was, as we have seen, when Arnold was in Philadelphia in 1774 as a representative from Connecticut to the First Continental Congress. Now, four years later, his military career was in full throttle. He had arrived in the city justly heralded for his courage and leadership under fire in Canada and at the decisive battles that led to the surrender of a large British army at Saratoga.

For her part, Peggy, now eighteen, had truly become a femme fatale seen as nearly irresistible by the many men who courted her favors. At first, she was a reluctant object of the widower's suit. Her father, the sometime-loyalist Edward Shippen, was anything but enthusiastic about the match. Eventually, however, both Peggy and her father relented; Arnold was, after all, a war hero with the major leadership position in their city. The couple was married on April 8, 1779, at a lavish ceremony at Judge Shippen's mansion.

Arnold now possessed what we call today would call a trophy wife; she was just the sort of lively beautiful woman he had always fancied and she offered just the social standing and graces he coveted. As for the Tory-leaning Shippens, they now had access to the top levels of power in the rebel cause that they so disliked. Also, it is important to what subsequently unfolds in this tale of intrigue to note that Peggy had a personal reason for resenting the American war against England. One of her closest friends, Theodora Prevost, had married a British officer and been widowed when he was killed in a battle with rebel forces. The grieving Theodora had become uncommonly virulent in her hatred of all things American and no doubt influenced Peggy to share her feelings.

In the event, the Shippens did not need to do much to fan the anger and growing inclination to disloyalty to the emerging United States in their new relative. The commander of Philadelphia was, by the time he married Peggy, deeply embroiled in the worst scandal of his life, a scandal that led to hatred of him throughout the city by British loyalists and American patriots alike. In April, 1779, eight formal charges of corruption and malfeasance in his office as commander were levied against him by the ruling Council of Pennsylvania. These included charges of obtaining illegal personal gain from two British ships, *Charming Nancy* and *Active*, which he had seized as booty without authorization from either General Washington or the council; using military wagons to transport personal property as booty; closing stores and shops in the city to everyone but himself for a week; favoring British loyalists in making appointments to city positions while generally treating patriots with disdain; and acting disrespectfully toward his civilian superiors in responding to their complaints against him.

When the charges against Arnold were brought before the Continental Congress, that body sought to avoid political controversy among its members by turning the matter over to the more vindictive Pennsylvania Council which disliked Arnold and was inclined to punish him. Most of the charges were frivolous and without merit, and probably none of them was judiciable. Arnold immediately appealed to Washington for a trial by his military peers, intemperately demanding that he be executed if found guilty.

Washington heeded the appeal.

Not until late in December did a full court-martial convene in Morristown, New Jersey. Major General Robert Howe of North Carolina presided over a trial board consisting of three brigadier generals and eight colonels. Arnold appeared in his own defense attired in full dress uniform. He read letters of commendation for his bravery from General Washington and deported himself in an arrogant style that virtually dared the court to find such a hero as himself guilty of anything.

On January 26, 1780, the court reached its verdict. Arnold was found guilty of his actions regarding the two British ships and their cargo, of transporting personal goods in military wagons and of the less serious charge of favoring loyalists over patriots in his administration of Philadelphia. The penalty was light: a reprimand from Washington. Congress approved the verdict within weeks. In April, Washington delivered the required reprimand, describing Arnold's behavior as "peculiarly reprehensible," "imprudent and "improper," but at the same time praising his military record.

Benedict Arnold and his new wife had already drawn their own conclusions. Long before the court-martial was even convened, probably shortly after the charges against him had been

referred by Congress to the Pennsylvania Council the previous
spring, the pair had reached their own verdict. They found
America guilty and proceeded to exact a fearful penalty on their
country.

Major John André
Courtesy of the Emmet Collection, Miriam and
Ira D. Wallach Division of Arts, Prints and Photographs,
The New York Public Library, Astor, Lenox and Tilden Foundations

Peggy Shippen Arnold at seventeen, drawn by John André
Courtesy of the Yale University Art Gallery

— CHAPTER 5 —

André the Spy

In mid-1779, while John Paulding was making his dramatic escape from Bayard's Sugar House Prison in New York and Benedict Arnold was in Philadelphia conspiring with his new wife, Peggy Shippen, to betray his country, the third principal actor in our drama, a young British officer named John André, was beginning his assignment on the staff of the new British commander in New York, General Sir Henry Clinton. André had recently been promoted to the post of deputy adjutant general with rank of major. His assignment was to organize and supervise British intelligence and espionage operations in New England and the mid-Atlantic states.

The handsome young major was arguably the most dashing, colorful, romantic, sympathetic and, ultimately, tragic figure in the entire saga of the American Revolution. As head of the extensive British spy network in the colonies, he was about to launch an undercover operation, secretly conceived and executed, which, if successful, would end the war by the end of the following year and produce rejoicing not only in England but with English sympathizers in America who numbered at least half of the population of the thirteen colonies.

Among the most influential of the Tory sympathizers upon whom André depended for intelligence and support was Judge Edward Shippen of Philadelphia. The Shippens were a Philadelphia dynasty, dating back to the days of William Penn and the founding of the city. They owned some of the best land in the city, were deeply involved it its politics and governance and were without peers among its intellectual and social elite. Their several homes were filled with books and fine art and all the accoutrements of high society.

To be sure, not all of the Shippens were British sympathizers. Dr. William Shippen, for example, was the chief medical officer of the Continental Army and Joseph was a lawyer and high official in city government who tried to remain neutral during the war. Judge Edward Shippen, however, was a known British sympathizer. By temperament, he was too shy and nervous to appear in court as a trial lawyer and so served as a judge of the Admiralty Court and in a variety of administrative posts in city government. He was nervous also about the war for independence, doubting both its wisdom and its prospects for success. Despite his lackluster professional performance and his failure to support the war effort, the judge was elevated after the war to the post of chief justice of the Pennsylvania Supreme Court. Such was the influence of the Shippen family.

Sympathy to England and a congenial cultural and social environment were not the only attractions that drew British officers like John André to Judge Shippen's fashionable residence on Fourth Street in Philadelphia during the British occupation of the city early in the war. There were also smart drawing room parties and lavish balls attended by the some of the most beautiful young women in the city including the judge's flirtatious daughters: Polly (Mary), Sally (Sarah), and the youngest, Peggy (Margaret) who was only in her mid-teens when André first met her in the winter of 1776. The major was immediately smitten. Peggy was already showing signs of the personality that would captivate many men, two of them fatally. She was, without doubt, one of the great *femme fatales* of American history, described by some as "a delectable creature," "a vital flame" and "flatteringly flirtatious" and regarded by others as spoiled, vain, flighty, conniving and vindictive.[20]

---

[20] Historians and biographers have given Peggy Shippen a mixed review. See esp. Anthony Bailey, *Major André*, New York, 1987, 26; Flexner, op.cit., 253 ff.; Van Doren, *Secret History of the American Revolution*, New York, 1941, 194; Wallace, op. cit., 195-6.

André, the Dilettante

André was an engaging, even irresistible, charmer—especially of women—though men were not oblivious to his winning ways. A Connecticut militiaman once described him as "the handsomest man I ever laid eyes on," and others responded, sometimes rhapsodically, to the wit, talent, affability, congeniality and good looks of the slender five-foot-nine dark-skinned Englishman.[21] His attractiveness was due in no small part to the fact that he expressed so much variety within a single personality; he was soldier, poet, artist, chronicler, dramatist, musician, brilliant conversationalist and all-around raconteur. He was at the same time boldly courageous and sensitively reticent, a good and loyal friend and a duplicitous liar. Even when caught by his enemies in the most ambivalent circumstance of his life, he would manage to win the sympathy and affection of many of them.[22]

From his earliest years John André was a striking mixture of promising elements. His father, Anthony, was a naturalized English citizen of French blood who had been born in Genoa into a prosperous family with business interests throughout Europe. He was raised and educated in Geneva and later married a French woman living in England. John was their first child, born in London in 1750 and baptized there in a French Protestant church. As his family grew to include three more children, Anthony moved to a country estate outside the city and took up life as an English gentleman of substantial means. Son John was sent to France to be educated. Here he became enamored of the arts. When he returned home at seventeen to begin his apprenticeship as heir apparent of the family's extensive business empire, he found the role intolerably incompatible with his artistic interests.

When his father died in 1769, nineteen-year-old John inherited a large portion of a substantial fortune that would come to him when he reached the age of twenty-one, only two years hence. He had already become part of the literary and artistic circle of the romantic poet, Anna Seward, at the spa town of Litchfield. Here

---

[21] Flexner, op. cit., 22.

[22] Extensive treatments of André's life and career are given in John Bakeless, *Turncoats, Traitors and Heroes*, New York, 1959 and Flexner, op. cit. See also, Van Doren, op. cit.; Bailey, op. cit.

he wrote poetry, painted and enjoyed the life of an artistic dilettante, far from his responsibilities to the family business. Soon he was indulging a romantic infatuation with Anna's ward, the beautiful Honora Speydt. When that affair ended, the young romantic abandoned the family business altogether and in January 1771 acquired an advance on his pending inheritance to seek adventure by buying a commission as a second lieutenant in the Royal Welsh Fusiliers.

Before long, André tired of military service and managed to inveigle extended leaves of absence from his regiment so that he could enroll in Gottinger University in Germany to study and write poetry as part of a group of romantics who idolized the ancient Teutonic knights and worshipped a moon goddess. Subsequently he wandered about Europe moving in and out of various artistic circles, now virtually a professional dilettante. Eventually, in the summer of 1774, he was forced to rejoin his unit, which had gone to fight in America. Even then, however, he was able to use family connections to assure a lengthy stop-over in that "most sophisticated of colonial Cities," Philadelphia, where he enjoyed the pleasures of the social and artistic life for a while before joining his regiment in Canada.

In the autumn of the year, André left Philadelphia to begin a leisurely overland journey to Quebec. Ever the writer and artist, he kept a detailed journal of the people he observed and the terrain he traversed en route through New York, Vermont and Maine, a journal filled with fine sketches and detailed comments on local customs and manners. In Quebec, he continued his writing about and sketching what for him was an exciting and exotic new environment, apparently preferring such pleasant diversions to the drudgery of military life. He was particularly struck by the Native Americans he encountered, finding them to be crude, uncouth and worthy of the mockery of his finely tuned intellectual sensibilities. But all of this genteel activity came to an abrupt end in September as the wealthy artiste-cum-soldier of fortune had his first encounter with the harsh reality of war.[23]

---

[23] For André's early years in Europe and England, see esp. Flexner, op. cit., 20-37.

"Prisoner of War"

His first battle was at St. Johns, just south of Montreal on the Sorel River that flowed northward from Lake Champlain in New York. It was a bloody affair in which he served as quartermaster for some 500 men, including some French Canadians and Native Americans under the command of Major John Preston. Even under the danger and stress of combat, André kept a detailed journal of the battle in which the British forces, although outnumbered by about four-to-one, were able to withstand the six-week American blockade, spearheaded by Colonel Benedict Arnold from Connecticut, before finally surrendering to General Richard Montgomery on November 3. By then the English governor general in Canada, Sir Guy Carleton, had left Montreal and fled to Quebec City.

Before the surrender, André had his first experience as British spy. He was dispatched by Preston to the American field command headquarters, ostensibly to negotiate terms of surrender but actually to spy on the enemy. His assignment was to make an assessment of American strength and of the prospect of the English forces receiving timely reinforcement from their troops then occupying the fortress at St. Johns. In the event, he was blindfolded by the Americans before being led into their headquarters. Once inside he was able to overhear what he thought to be accurate corroboration from a captured French Canadian to the effect that there would be no reinforcements coming to aid the English.

In his journal André described the American army during the subsequent surrender ceremonies as slovenly and undisciplined in contrast with the smartly dressed and sharply arrayed men of his own unit who accepted defeat like the gentlemen they were. Not for the first time, the cultivated English snob read outward manners as the measure of the true character of his American foes. In fact, the behavior of the victors at St. Johns was all that the most fastidious European gentlemen of the day might expect. The vanquished soldiers were congratulated publicly for their valor and trusted to keep their words of honor to refrain from further combat when released. The officers were allowed to retain their swords and to travel without escort to the various places where they were to remain without supervision under a kind of "house arrest" until either the end of the war or their release in a subsequent prisoner exchange. With ungracious and dishonest petulance, André recorded that most of these courtesies were not extended and that his captors were altogether uncouth and barbarous ruffians.

Regardless of what André wanted posterity to think about these uncivilized Americans, he was in fact trusted to travel under his own recognizance to his designated place of confinement, Lancaster, Pennsylvania. He took his time getting there, once again chronicling the people and scenery as he journeyed southward. One night, while trying unsuccessfully to sleep under a shared blanket on the floor of an overcrowded inn on the shore of Lake George, he engaged his charming floor-mate in intellectual conversation until dawn. That gentleman was none other then Colonel Henry Knox, on his way north under orders from General Washington to seize the cannon at Fort Ticonderoga, an outpost that General Benedict Arnold had captured some months earlier, and by some means or other to drag them through the rough winter weather to Boston.

Stopping for a few weeks at Albany, André stayed in the mansion owned by General Philip Schuyler, the commander of the very forces that had captured him at St. Johns. He also paid a call on Abraham Cuyler, the mayor of Albany and did a sketch of his wife. Traveling on down the Hudson in early January of 1776, he stopped at Haverstraw and had dinner with a colonel in the New York militia. Also at dinner was a young man by the name of Joshua Hett Smith whom André thought to be little more than a dandy but who would later figure fatefully in his life.

Finally, André arrived back in his beloved Philadelphia and, although supposedly a prisoner of war, launched himself at once into the glittering social scene he had so much enjoyed a year and a half earlier. Here he unpacked his books, sketch pad and flute and proceeded to flirt with, charm and sketch some of the Tory-leaning ladies of the city, including an intense, moody and beguiling fifteen-year-old blonde beauty named Peggy Shippen.

Within a few months, however, he had to leave all of this behind, finally arriving in the remote town of Lancaster, Pennsylvania, and settling into his "imprisonment."

Not surprisingly, André, ever the English gentleman, found this town to be a depressed, inhospitable backwater with few redeeming qualities. Despite his best efforts to cultivate the few congenial literary souls in town and distract himself by giving drawing lessons to aspiring young artists, he found the anti-British attitudes threatening. Surely he would have left had he not given his word of honor to remain in a place that was indeed a prison to him. His situation only worsened when the American command decided to further disperse captured officers in order to prevent them from organizing and leading captured soldiers into escape. He was ordered to repair to the even more remote town of Carlisle. Here André and his fellow captives were reviled and hated by the rough provincials, often abused both verbally and physically. This experience colored André's view of Americans from that time forward, intensifying his feeling that these colonials were little more than barbarians and deserved to be treated as such by their betters from England.

In late November of 1776, a massive prisoner exchange was arranged allowing André to leave Carlisle and proceed to the British base at New Brunswick whence he might have gone home with his fellow prisoners. Instead, now quite aroused by an apparently visceral hostility to what he regarded as the ignorant and ignoble Americans, he decided to stay on and offer himself as an aide to General Howe. The British commander welcomed the brilliant young officer to his staff and in June of 1777, appointed him as aide-de-camp to newly arrived General Charles Grey. That officer soon inaugurated a vicious "burn and kill" campaign designed to discourage civilians from aiding the local militia and to encourage rebel soldiers to lay down their arms and go home.

At Large in America

André found the approach of the ruthless Grey much to his liking. He fought bravely at the bloody Battle of Brandywine in September and participated enthusiastically in the horrible Paoli Massacre a few days later, joining Grey and others in bayoneting civilians and prisoners alike. Not long after that grizzly attack, André fought in the Battle of Germantown, commanding troops from horseback while waving his sword in the air as his horse was shot out from under him. He seemed to be acting out all of his romantic ideas about gallant knights waging a just war against the infidels. Remember, here was a man who once followed a Teutonic moon goddess cult.

Arriving in Philadelphia in time for the winter social season, André spent his time flitting about from one parlor to another, playing his music, writing and reading poetry, painting scenery, writing dialogue and sometimes acting as a member of a group called Howe's Thespians. He attended balls, dancing and flirting with the lovely ladies of the city. His favorite was the beautiful Peggy Chew with whom he was passionately in love. But there were others as well, including the sultry young Peggy Shippen. André may well have had sexual affairs with both of his Peggys as well as others. Certainly there was outrageous flirting and expressive language used by the partners in describing their "affairs," but one must be cautious about drawing final conclusions in such matters as the social conventions of the day in Philadelphia were not those of Paris, or even London. Here, society still frowned on actually consummating romantic relations outside of marriage.

In November of 1777, General Howe offered his resignation as commander in America to King George III. He was allowed to leave Philadelphia and return home as soon as Sir Henry Clinton relieved him the following spring. Howe's officers were fond of their commander and decided to throw an elaborate ball in his honor before he departed. Because it would involve a variety of entertainments, including dancing, jousting, competitions for the favor of certain young women, fireworks, an enormous banquet and much more, it was called the *Meshianza* (*Mischinaza*) or a "variety ball." Never before had such an event been seen in Philadelphia.

André and his fellow officers contributed the huge sum of £3,000 to pay for decorating a gigantic hall and underwriting other costs. Some of the most attractive and wealthy young women in the city were invited to attend so long as they were dressed as medieval Turkish maidens garbed in the finest silks and exotic beads and sporting elaborate hair styles created for them by none other than Major André. These ladies would ever thereafter be referred to as "the *Meshianza* Ladies." The men came as knights, outfitted in medieval armor. An English silk shop in the city is reported to have sold £12,000 worth of cloth and accessories for the ladies' gowns. Some of their fathers, including Edward Shippen, whose three daughters had all been invited, were appalled at the horrendous costs involved.

For many weeks, André threw himself enthusiastically into planning and managing all details of this exotic ball. When the big event came, he escorted his favorite, Peggy Chew. A deeply embittered and disappointed Peggy Shippen was not in attendance because her father had yielded to the protestations of a group of Quakers who entreated him in the name of all decency not to be involved in such an ostentatious, pagan and unpatriotic display.

Not long after the ball, Clinton replaced Howe and promptly evacuated Philadelphia in order to concentrate his forces in New York City. André followed the new commander, eager to curry his favor and continue his rise in rank and influence in the king's army. Peggy Shippen, Peggy Chew and the other rich young women of Philadelphia were left behind, bereft of the excitement of the dazzling social life provided by the dashing, romantic British officers, Major John André paramount among them.

Despite the loss of his major military patrons, Generals Howe and Grey, he managed successfully to cultivate the prickly Clinton and soon became one of the new commander's principal aides in the thoroughly corrupt British occupation government in New York City. Indeed, in the midst of the maze of inefficiency and venality of Clinton's government, André stood out as a bright star—a clear-thinking, efficient, responsive and charming officer to whom one could go for solutions to the myriad problems of trying to conduct business in this almost hopelessly dishonest military government. At the very least, André could be relied upon to tell important citizens which official they needed to bribe in order to advance their interests.

Along with his roles as unofficial ombudsman and liaison, André pursued an active social life and continued his artistic and literary interests while in New York. As in Philadelphia, he was a frequent guest at glittering balls and receptions. He wrote poetry, sketched some of the wealthy ladies and their important spouses, and painted scenery and composed prologues for a variety of dramatic productions in the city.

Top-Notch Top Secret

André's most important assignment under Clinton was, as noted, to serve as chief of British intelligence operations. André's spies performed two essential missions: to gather information about rebel troop deployments and fortifications and to discern who among American leaders might be inclined to defect or at least to disrupt the lives and threaten the welfare of their fellow citizens. Sowing disunity, even to the point of fomenting civil war, and encouraging defections among military and civilian leaders, were major parts of British strategy.

To facilitate spying, an elaborate clandestine system of communication was developed including codes in invisible inks that were revealed by application of heat or certain chemicals. Often the codes involved the substitution of numbers for letters or their use to designate column and word orders in specified dictionaries that would spell out the secret dispatch. Sometimes simpler codes were employed merely substituting names of famous people and places for those intended: for example, "Rome" was Carlisle; "the Jordan" was the Susquehanna River; "Gomorrah" was Fort Pitt; "Synagogue" was Congress; "James" was George Washington; "Matthew" was General Sullivan.[24]

A steady flow of information reached André in New York, not only from his spies in the field but also from the stream of loyalist citizens fleeing to the safety of British lines from angry neighbors, bands of raiding parties and the colonial militia to the safety of the British lines. André knew virtually everything that Washington and his officers were doing, often before they did it. He had an extensive list of possible defectors including a number of high-ranking generals. Notably absent from his list was General Benedict Arnold, who was deemed too loyal to the colonial cause to be a target for treason.

Among the most notable of the many spies in André's employ was Anne Bates, described by one historian as "one of the most remarkable female agents" in all of history.[25] Anne Bates was a

---

[24] Bakeless, op. cit., 269-70.
[25] Ibid., 267.

Philadelphia schoolteacher married to an English soldier. She kept bees and ran a little shop to make ends meet until she followed the British when they left Philadelphia for New York. As early as June 1778 she was engaged in critical spying, posing as a peddler selling medicines, knives, needles and thread and other miscellany. Peddling was a typical ruse for André's spies. Bates moved easily through the neutral ground and behind American lines gathering information as she went. To identify herself to English loyalists, she carried a token of some sort that they would recognize to signify that she was one of their own.

Bates was so effective that she even walked right into various command headquarters, including Washington's, gathering information simply by listening to conversations or asking supposedly innocent questions. As she traveled into rebel territory, she stayed each night in one of many "spy houses" where loyalist citizens provided safe haven for the English agents working in the Hudson River Valley region. She was amazingly courageous and resourceful, surviving narrow escapes, outwitting would-be captors and displaying audacious bravery as she ran great personal risks. She often sought out loyalists to gather information for her in places she was unable to enter herself. At the end of the war, despite having turned over much vital information to André and Clinton, she was still a free woman.

Whenever the Americans captured any of André's agents who concealed their identities by wearing disguises, especially those who were members of the British military not in uniform, they tried and executed them quickly. In one such instance Andrew Patchen, a British soldier out of uniform, was caught buying beef for his troops within American lines. He was hanged by General Israel Putman himself when the executioner lost his nerve.

In May of 1779, not long after André took charge of the intelligence system, a loyalist tradesman in New York by the name of Joseph Stansbury contacted General Benedict Arnold, who was at the time Washington's military commander in Philadelphia, about the benefits of selling military information and perhaps even defecting. Despite André's suppositions, Arnold was interested in the possibility. When André received the coded messages to this effect from Stansbury, he developed a special code for communicating with the American general.

But, at the time, Clinton was not interested in Arnold's offer of defection because he felt that the payments demanded by the American were exorbitant and also because Arnold was a disgraced officer without significant command who really had nothing much of value to offer beyond the symbolic victory of securing his defection. Clinton told André that perhaps some time in the future, if Arnold could secure command of some important fortress or at least access to vital military information, an arrangement might be reached.

In his reply to Arnold, André said that in future he would not correspond directly with him but only through Arnold's new wife, whom André knew very well, perhaps even intimately. She was, of course, none other than Peggy Shippen, now Peggy Arnold.

CHAPTER 6

The Patriot, the Traitor and the Spy

Following his dramatic escape from the Sugar House Prison in New York City, John Paulding returned to his farm east of Tarrytown, continuing to serve in the local militia on special spying and foraging assignments. By the summer of 1780, he was a sergeant in the company of Lieutenant Daniel Peacock whose unit was attached to the Westchester volunteer militia.

The Patriot Poised

In September, while on patrol north of Tarrytown near Bedford, Paulding's unit was spotted by a British patrol on its way back to New York. Outnumbered by about five to one by Captain Totten's detachment of horsemen, Paulding and his companions engaged in a fierce but futile battle. Along with twenty of his fellows, he was imprisoned once again, this time at North Dutch Church in lower Manhattan where hundreds of prisoners were incarcerated within a compound surrounded by a high fence. Here he was held for about three weeks.[26]

After careful planning, the intrepid twenty year old arranged to have fellow prisoners create a diversion by fighting in the yard. While the guards were distracted, he climbed onto a box, leaped high in the air, grabbed the top of the fence and hauled himself up and over and down the other side. He now found himself in a small yard where there was a young woman minding the gate that opened onto the street outside. He asked her to open the gate. "Are

---

[26] For accounts of this capture and escape see Patterson, op. cit., 137; Meade, op. cit., 277; John Evangelist Walsh, *The Execution of Major André*, New York, 2001, 99-100.

you one of the prisoners?" she asked. "Yes," was his answer, whereupon she opened the gate and he walked outside. Paulding had arranged with a black woman who lived in a small hut next to the prison and came into the compound regularly to sell fruit to the prisoners to have her hide him. Paulding ran to her house and laid low in her cellar for the night.

Almost at once, the prisoner's absence was noticed. A search was conducted within the compound and the precincts in the immediate vicinity. A young man who resembled Paulding was apprehended, brought into the prison and "beaten unmercifully before the truth of the matter was discovered." Next day Paulding sneaked uptown to the house of a friend, who hid him overnight, gave him food, money and a green Hessian coat trimmed in red as a disguise to get him out of the city and through British lines. He fled westward to the river, found a small boat, crossed the Hudson and walked northward to the American base at Tappan. From there he re-crossed the river and finally arrived home in Tarrytown where he immediately rejoined his unit.[27]

Four days later, on September 23, 1780, Paulding, still wearing his Hessian jacket, had joined a deployment of seven voluntary militiamen under a Sergeant John Yerkes of the First Westchester Militia serving under general command of Captain Baker of Sheldon's Regiment of Dragoons. He was in the woods along the Albany Post Road near Tarrytown where Cowboys had been raiding the day before. At this point, voluntary militiamen, like Paulding and his compatriots, had an express commission to look for and intercept Cowboys, Tory sympathizers or British patrols that happened to pass along the road. They would be rewarded for turning in any booty they might take from the enemy in the form of confiscated livestock, crops or other valuables. The New York Provincial Legislature had specifically authorized

---

[27] Some accounts have Paulding captured as a spy by American forces at Tappan but later released by Lafayette. See Patterson, op., cit., 137. I prefer the near eye-witness account of Alexander Boyce that places this event during his first escape a year before.

payment of one-half the value of any loot seized by volunteer militia or Skinners.[28]

Paulding positioned himself near a bridge that spanned Clark's Kill, a small tributary of the Croton River, to lay in wait for any unwary passersby. He was accompanied by two of his fellow volunteers, twenty-five-year-old David Williams and twenty-one-year-old Isaac Van Wart. The other four members of the troop, Paulding's cousin, James Romer, John Dean, Abraham Williams and Isaac See, stationed themselves atop a hill overlooking nearby Bedford Road. David Williams had joined the group specifically to avenge the killing of a neighbor just a few days earlier.

Each of the three men hiding near the bridge in the bushes that morning carried his own gun. None was garbed in a regulation military uniform. Williams and Van Wart wore the typical civilian clothes of yeoman farmers of the day: brown tunics, knee britches, stockings and cocked hats. Paulding wore his green Jaeger jacket, laced with red trim, the same one that he had used as a disguise during his escape from prison just a few days earlier—the jacket typically worn by the Hessian mercenaries employed by the British.

Thus was John Paulding ready for his appointment with destiny: a tall, husky, close-cropped, rough-looking, twenty-two-year-old farmer, a scarcely respectable relative of the prominent Pauldings of Tarrytown and New York, just out of prison and already fully engaged in the dangerous and adventurous life of an opportunistic Robin Hood, seeking his fortune in the dangerous neutral ground while at the same time serving, after his own fashion, the cause of American independence. In just a few moments something would happen on the road in front of him that would forever alter his life and that of his country.

---

[28] That such volunteer units as Paulding's were officially sanctioned and not outlaw bands of opportunistic raiders is the opinion of most historians. See esp. Charles H. Roe, "André's Captors," *Westchester Historian*, Fall, 1966, 62-5. Historians more sympathetic to Arnold and André have been inclined to credit André's and Arnold's versions of major events and taken a contrary view of Paulding's motives. See, for example, Wallace, op. cit., 244-5; Harry M. Ward, *Between the Lines*, New York, 2002, 27; Charles Hall, *Benjamin Tallmadge: Revolutionary Soldier and American Businessman*, New York, 1943, 60.

A Traitor's Treachery

The first clear signal, in hindsight, that Benedict Arnold had made his fateful decision to betray his country and sell out to the British came with the moment when he declined Washington's offer to command the left wing of the northern army. That plum was tendered just prior to Arnold's court-martial at Morristown. There could be no greater evidence of Washington's continued confidence in his sometime-discredited general than his offer of just the sort of command Arnold had always coveted, and doing so at this critical point in Arnold's career.

One can imagine Washington's dismay when Arnold rejected the position and asked instead for the command of the fortress at West Point. This was the sort of back-water administrative job that Arnold had always disparaged and avoided. So far as we know, Washington never suspected his subordinate's true motive in seeking the West Point post. On August 3, 1780, Arnold assumed command of West Point and the other nearby forts and redoubts[29] along both banks of the Hudson.

As early as the previous spring, Peggy Arnold had supported, if not encouraged, her husband's inclination to see what terms he might arrange if he decided to defect. She urged him to contact a loyalist named Joseph Stansbury who owned a glass and china shop in Philadelphia and had the ear of Sir Henry Clinton and the British command in New York. For a time, Arnold concealed his identity, communicating through Stansbury only as an anonymous general seeking to defect if satisfactory terms could be arranged. Clinton's new aide, John André, quickly divined Arnold's identity and Peggy then began to send messages directly to her old friend who was by this time the head of Clinton's extensive spying and espionage network.[30]

---

[29] Redoubts are small defensive fortifications designed to protect a specific piece of ground and located within or near a larger fort.

[30] That Peggy Shippen Arnold was a major factor in Arnold's treason is an improvable but likely theory, based on circumstantial evidence but advanced by most historians. Writers of fiction have enjoyed telling a

Before long, Arnold was using one of several elaborate secret codes devised by André[31] to entice Clinton with classified information concerning troop movements, sensitive financial data, political developments in Congress and the military high command and the current status of relations between the Americans and French. But the English commander was not impressed. He already possessed much of Arnold's information through other channels. Furthermore, he was well aware that Arnold was currently in disgrace with no good prospects for an important command.

In July, Arnold sent information on troop deployments, along with a demand for payment of £10,000 regardless of the outcome of the war. Peggy ("Mrs. Moore"), in the same message, placed an order for "silk and other rich materials" some of it in "pink color." (Was this a legitimate request from the always acquisitive Peggy who saw a chance for some nice luxuries unattainable at West Point or was it too part of the code? We don't know.) Clinton demurred on all counts. Through André, he replied that he would not pay the £10,000 unless and until he received more detailed information on American fortifications along the Hudson, especially at West Point, plus some assurance that Arnold was in a position to surrender most of these forts to him. This would require that Arnold be in command at West Point. If this were to happen, Clinton would be willing to negotiate with the American.[32]

Shortly before the April 1780 guilty verdict in his court-martial trial, Arnold, with a clear eye on Clinton's demand that he have something of worth to deliver, contacted his friend General Philip Schuyler seeking his help in convincing Washington to give him an important command along the Hudson, preferably at West Point. While waiting for Washington's reply, Arnold sent more confidential information to Clinton in June. This time it concerned plans of the French, under Lafayette, to attack the British from Canada with a joint French-Canadian force of some 8,000 troops.

story that paints Peggy as a femme fatale villain. See Ann Rinaldi, *Finishing Becca*, New York, 1994.
[31] Bakeless, op. cit., 269-70, 280-81; Van Doren, op. cit., 200.
[32] Ibid., 209-10.

When Clinton's reply to this information was less than enthusiastic, Arnold was enraged. He sent back a coded message on July 15, saying that he now had command of West Point (which he did not) and expected immediate payment of £10,000 (about $33,000 in the currency of the time, or $450,000 in today's money) as a life annuity and another £20,000 ($66,000, or close to one million dollars in the currency of 2005) when he delivered West Point. Furthermore, he expected a full and immediate reply to his demand. The traitor's patience with the British was exhausted.[33]

In his reply, Clinton told Arnold that he would pay him £20,000 for West Point. Earlier in the month, Washington had finally given Arnold command at West Point and so, at last, he was in a position to consummate his treason. While these negotiations were going forward, Arnold, not lacking in hubris, had demanded money from Congress for what he claimed was owed him for back salary, as well as a cash advance to buy equipment for his new post. Congress ignored the claim for back pay but did authorize $25,000 for the equipment.[34]

Shortly after his appointment to West Point on the third of August, Arnold moved his headquarters and his family across the river into the home of Colonel Beverly Robinson. The new commander had no intention of being at the fort itself when the British breached its defenses and seized it. Although Colonel Robinson's father had been a friend of Washington's and had served as speaker of the Virginia colonial legislature, the Robinsons had remained loyal to the British when war broke out. By then, Beverly Robinson had married a wealthy heiress who

---

[33] It is, of course, very risky to estimate such values over the centuries. Many variables are involved including the difficulty of determining the value of money during eighteenth century America when it was often virtually worthless. Another problem of enormous magnitude is that such comparisons must always be made in terms of the purchasing power of money, and there is infinitely more available for purchase in the twenty-first century than in the eighteenth. All this said, I am reasonably confidant that my estimates are close enough to provide the twenty-first-century reader some idea of what Arnold was asking, namely an amount that would seem worthy of what he was promising to deliver.

[34] Van Doren, op. cit., 275.

owned a large estate overlooking the Hudson River in Duchess County. He lived the life of a gentleman of leisure and wealth, a neutral in the war who offered his home and his good offices to American and English generals alike.

When Colonel Robinson was required to take an oath of allegiance to the new nation, he refused and had to move his home behind British lines to a house on the east side of the Hudson. Here he declared his full loyalty to the royalist cause by raising local troops to fight for the British in a regiment called the Loyal Americans. Robinson also engaged in spying activities, keeping Clinton informed on American troop movements in the region. He was, in fact, André's chief operative for coordinating intelligence activities in and around West Point. When the Americans took over the east side of the river across from West Point, Robinson had to leave again, abandoning his house to the rebels. It was to his house that Arnold planned to repair once he turned traitor. Throughout the war, Robinson nevertheless tried to remain circumspect and cautious in his loyalist activities and to maintain good social relationships with a few of the high officers in the American army. He was the ideal loyalist civilian to arrange high-level secret negotiations if they should ever be needed.[35]

The Spy Sprung

While Benedict Arnold and his wife Peggy were busily arranging the details of their treason and settling into the Robinson house during the summer of 1780, John André was in New York planning his meeting with Arnold. Both his military and artistic persona had been on full display that summer and autumn. In September he was promoted to adjutant general on Clinton's staff with full access to the British commander and virtual control over all military intelligence and espionage. He had realistic hopes of actually commanding the final and decisive victory over the rebels by leading forces up the river to capture West Point and control the vital Hudson Valley route to Canada.

---

[35] Edward Boynton, *History of West Point and its Military Importance during the American Revolution*, New York, 1863, 98.

His artistic work continued to occupy much of his time. He
completed a satirical poem called "The Cow Chase"—a work in
three cantos, with seventy-one stanzas of four lines each—in
which he depicted and celebrated the British victory at Bulls
Ferry, New Jersey. In the piece he denigrated Americans and their
way of life. On display was the snobbish disdain that had become
characteristic of his attitude toward all things American. He
referred to rebel soldiers as members of "dung-born tribes." The
poem named names on both sides of the conflict and deplored the
rebels for destroying ties of "friendship and love" and every other
"genial bond." One stanza read: "Oh cursed rebellion! these are
thine/Thine are these tales of woe/Shall at thy dire insatiate shrine
Blood never cease to flow?" André left the poem with a printer
just before he departed on his fateful trip upriver to meet General
Arnold. Ironically, it appeared in the *Royal Gazette* on the very
day of the denouement of his American adventure at a small river
crossing near Tarrytown.[36]

The journey upriver from New York through the dangerous
neutral ground and finally into rebel-held territory to negotiate in
secret with Arnold was just the sort of romantic adventure that
appealed to André's sense of the heroic. He planned the details for
weeks in secret correspondence with the American general. At the
end of August, Arnold wrote to him, using an imperious third-
person voice, to insist that his demands for money and rank were
not unreasonable and that he expected to be paid in cash the
moment he delivered his information:

> He is still of the opinion that his first proposal was by no
> means unreasonable, and makes no doubt, when he has
> conference with you, that you will close with it. He expects,
> when you meet, that you will be fully authorized from your
> house; that the risks and profits of the co-partnership may
> be fully understood. A speculation of this kind might be
> easily made with ready money.[37]

---

[36] William Dunlap, *André: A Tragedy in Five Acts*, New York, 1798, 79;
Van Doren, op., cit., 321.

[37] B. J. Lossing, *Pictoral Fieldbook of the Revolution*, New York, 1851,
715. See also, Boynton, op. cit., 93-94.

Arnold went on to propose that he and André meet at the home of Colonel Beverly Robinson, which had become Arnold's headquarters. The message sent, he then informed Colonel Elisha Sheldon, his troop commander on the east side of the Hudson, that a man from New York would be appearing some evening soon bearing vital information from the enemy. This person should be granted safe passage through American lines and brought directly to him.

André responded somewhat negatively to Arnold's letter in a coded message to Colonel Sheldon carried into rebel territory by one of his couriers. Signing his message "John Anderson," André informed Sheldon that he did not think it safe to come behind American lines and would prefer instead to meet Arnold in the neutral ground at Dobbs Ferry. André wrote:

> I am told that my name is made known to you, and that I may hope your indulgence in permitting me to meet a friend near your outposts. I will endeavor to obtain permission to go out with a flag [of truce] which will be sent to Dobbs Ferry Monday next, the 11th instant at twelve o'clock, when I shall be happy to meet Mr. G_____. Should I not be allowed to go, the officer who is to command the escort— between whom and my self no distinction need be made— can speak in the affair.[38]

Colonel Sheldon forwarded the message immediately to Arnold, rightly surmising that "John Anderson" was the man referred to in their earlier communication. In the event, Arnold went down to Haverstraw on September 10 and spent the night with a leading American patriot, Joshua Hett Smith. Next morning Arnold took a river barge down to Dobbs Ferry toward the place along the shore where André said he and Colonel Robinson would be waiting for him aboard the British ship, *Vulture*. Realizing that Washington, then staying in Bergen County, New Jersey, might have observed his trip down river to Dobbs Ferry, Arnold sent his commander-in-chief a message providing plausible reasons for such a journey:

---

[38] Lossing, op. cit.

I came here [Dobbs Ferry] this morning in order to establish signals, to be observed in case the enemy came up the river; to give some directions, respecting guard-boats; and to have a beacon fixed upon the mountain, above about five miles south of Kin's Ferry, that will be necessary to alarm the country.[39]

In one of those incredible failures of communication that seem almost to characterize warfare, all of these elaborate machinations came to nothing. Officers on American gunboats patrolling that region of the Hudson had not been told that a British ship coming upriver had a safe conduct. They opened fire and drove *The Vulture* back down the river, thereby unwittingly foiling the Arnold-André plot—at least for a time.

Arnold contra *Washington*

The very next day, September 11, Washington stopped at West Point to visit Arnold and ask his subordinate to accompany him to his headquarters at Peekskill. Once there, Arnold sent a coded message to his fellow conspirator, Colonel Robinson, telling him that he would be sending someone to meet "Mr. Anderson" again, this time on the night of September 20.

Several days later, an annoyed General Arnold was with his wife, who had just left Philadelphia and accepted the hospitality of Joshua Hett Smith. That gentleman had invited the Arnolds for an extended stay at his house in Haverstraw. Smith was a prominent citizen who lived in a large house fronting the river about two and a half miles below Stony Point. Affording magnificent views of Haverstraw Bay and Teller's Point, his home was a frequent location for meetings and social gatherings of Hudson Valley notables. Smith had served in the New York Provisional Congress and was an interesting type one sees occasionally in wartime who seems to thrive on the excitement of working at the highest levels for both sides. He had done some spying for the Americans; however, he was known to be opposed to the Revolution and had

---

[39] Jared Sparks, *The Correspondence of the American Revolution*, Boston, 1853, 81.

also worked for the British from time to time, including sending them badly needed supplies. His demeanor was unfailingly courteous and accommodating, making him an ideal person to engage in intelligence work for either side.

Smith's fence-straddling was to make him an ideally pivotal character in Arnold's strategy of betrayal because he was regarded as an acceptable and useful, if not altogether trusted, character by both camps. We shall see later how his service for Arnold during Arnold's meeting with Major André was to be rewarded.[40]

From Smith's house, on September 13, Arnold wrote again to André, telling him that he would be met by a reliable person (Smith) just a week hence within rebel territory on the east side of the river opposite Dobbs Ferry.

> It will be necessary for you to be in disguise. I can be no more explicit at present. Meet me if possible. You may rest assured that, if there is no danger passing your lines, you will be perfectly safe where I propose a meeting.[41]

In this same communication, Arnold sent confidential intelligence for André to pass on to Clinton, information he had just received directly from Washington about an upcoming secret meeting at Hartford, Connecticut, between Washington and the French General Compt de Rochambeau and Admiral Chavalier de Ternay. Included in this message was the exact location (King's Point) at which Washington would be landing after crossing the river on Sunday, September 17 and where he would be lodging that night on his way to the Hartford meeting (Peekskill). The American commander would surely be vulnerable to capture now that the British knew his exact itinerary, especially when and where he would be crossing the river. Arnold's treachery peaked as he rushed this intelligence to André. Here was a prize he had probably never hoped to be able to deliver: Washington himself! Surely his reward would be great indeed.[42]

What makes Arnold's betrayal so complete is that Washington, trusting him wholly, had given him alone the

---

[40] Boynton, op. cit., 101-02.

[41] Lossing, op. cit., 717.

[42] Ibid.

information about his movements, asking him personally to arrange a guard consisting "of a captain and about 50 men" with "a forage for about 40 horses" to escort him out of West Point and across the river to Peekskill, where he would spend the night before moving on to Hartford the next day. Washington had specifically asked Arnold "to keep this to yourself as I want to make my journey a secret."[43]

On September 18, Arnold, now primed with the prospect of delivering Washington to the British, wrote again to André with the information that a few days after André's return to New York from their upcoming meeting, Washington would be visiting Arnold at his headquarters in Colonel Robinson's house. If Admiral Rodney's squadron sailed quickly from New York, they would be at West Point in twelve hours and could capture Washington while seizing the fort.

At about the same time that he sent this letter to André, Arnold wrote to Major Benjamin Talmadge, the commander at North Castle, ordering him to bring "John Anderson" directly to him should he encounter that gentleman on the twentieth or twenty-first. He wrote also to Colonel Robinson asking him to send someone to pick up André when he arrived aboard the British sloop *Vulture* under a flag of truce. He sent a copy of this letter to Sir Henry Clinton in New York.

Further weaving his intricate plot, just before Washington left for Hartford Arnold showed him a letter he had received from Colonel Robinson inviting him to use his house as a headquarters. Washington replied that Arnold was to cut off any relationship with Robinson because he was a Tory loyalist and not to be trusted. This gave Arnold the excuse he needed to send a courier to his co-conspirator, Robinson, who was already aboard *The Vulture* as his agent. In that letter, Arnold did not, of course, follow Washington's advice but, instead, furthered his treasonous plot by informing his accomplice that he was sending an unwitting representative, Joshua Smith, to bring "Mr. Anderson" ashore.[44]

---

[43] Van Doren, op. cit., 314; Patterson, op. cit., 120.

[44] Patterson, op. cit.

Traitor and Spy

Meanwhile, a few days before his trip upriver, André had been briefed by Clinton on his mission. He was ordered to talk to no one but Arnold, whom Clinton assumed would come out to *The Vulture* and escort him to Robinson's house. The danger was great. If André was captured as a spy, he would be certainly executed. However, if seen as an emissary between the two sides, his passage would be allowed. Thus, he should travel in uniform under a flag of truce and if apprehended he could say that he was only carrying a coded message between the opposing commanders. Furthermore, Clinton instructed, André was not to go inside enemy lines and not to accept any papers or other items from Arnold that might identify him as a spy.[45]

On the afternoon of September 20, André, in the guise of "John Anderson," arrived on schedule at Dobbs Ferry on a ship from New York. At about 7:00 p.m. he boarded *The Vulture* at Tellers Point to await the arrival of Arnold or his representative. But no one arrived. Sometime after midnight on the morning of the September 21 a message was sent ashore under a flag of truce from the ship's captain and co-signed by his "secretary," "John Anderson." When this message was delivered to Arnold he was certain at last that André was aboard *The Vulture.*

But Arnold had no intention of running the risk of going out to *The Vulture* and personally escorting André to shore. Instead, he asked his friend and neighbor, Joshua Hett Smith, to take a small boat out to the British sloop and bring "John Anderson" to his house where Arnold would be waiting for him. He told the unwitting Smith that "Anderson" was a merchant from New York with whom he had private business to conduct.

No doubt Smith, who had facilitated other clandestine missions for both the British and the Americans, doubted Arnold's cover story and suspected that the general might be having a secret meeting with a representative from the British, although, so far as is known, Arnold never revealed to him the identity of "John Anderson" or the reason for his visit. Arnold did, however, give Smith the impression that he was doing a great service to the

---

[45] Lossing, op. cit., 718-19.

revolutionary cause by facilitating a meeting between the commander at West Point and a British agent.[46]

On the morning of September 21, Arnold gave Smith a safe conduct pass and a letter to Major Edward Kierse at Stony Point ordering his subordinate to give Smith a boat and a boatman to carry him out to *The Vulture* to pick up "Mr. Anderson." Smith had gone with his family to visit friends at nearby Fishkill so that his house was now vacant and available for the secret meeting between Arnold and André scheduled for that night or early the next morning. Meantime, Arnold had moved his wife and new baby son out of Smith's house, where they been temporarily lodged since their trip from Philadelphia, and into their new home and headquarters across the river at the Beverly Robinson house.

The entire plan to meet with André almost collapsed again when neither Major Kierse nor Joshua Smith could find any boatmen willing to obey Arnold's order to row Smith out to *The Vulture* and pick up "Mr. Anderson." Finally, Arnold himself threatened Smith's two tenants, the Cohoon brothers, with serious consequences unless they took their landlord out into the river on this errand. And so, on the calm clear night of September 21, 1780, just after midnight, Smith set out into the river to meet a man named "Mr. Anderson" whom he probably assumed was carrying important information from Sir Henry Clinton to General Benedict Arnold—perhaps word of terms for surrender or at least an offer of withdrawal by the British.

Once aboard *The Vulture*, Smith handed Colonel Robinson, who had come aboard earlier to greet André on behalf of Arnold, a message from Arnold that read in part:

> This will be delivered to you by Mr. Smith, who will conduct you to a place of safety. Neither Mr. Smith nor any other person shall be made acquainted with your proposals. If they (which I doubt not) are of such a nature that I can officially take notice of them, I shall do it with pleasure. I take it for granted that Colonel Robinson will not propose

---

[46] Patterson, op. cit.,

anything that is not for the interest of the United States as well as himself.[47]

André, realizing that the tone of the coded message was intended to protect Robinson from possible detection by Smith as a co-conspirator, put on a blue coat and cape over his red British coat, got into the small boat with Smith and was promptly rowed ashore by the two oarsmen. He was deposited in a secluded spot near the river on "the edge of a fir wood at the foot of Long Clove Mountain below Haverstraw." Smith then went in search of Arnold. Finding the general waiting nearby, he brought him to André and then withdrew so that the two men could talk privately.[48]

The spy and the traitor talked for several hours in the darkness amongst the trees along the river bank about terms of Arnold's defection, which despite all that had been risked, were still to be determined. Arnold revealed to André his plan for Clinton to sail from New York with a large force. When he came upriver he would find that the chain across the Hudson had been replaced with a rope and that the total force of 3,000 men would be immediately surrendered to him. Arnold also gave the British major vital military information, including details on the best methods to use in capturing Fort Putnam and the exact deployment of American troops at the forts. As the two conspirators continued their negotiations, André was delighted that Arnold was giving him even more than he had expected.[49]

Unfortunately, much of what Arnold had was in the written form that Clinton had told André not to accept, rightly fearing that if his adjutant was caught by the Americans with anything in writing, he would be executed as a spy. In the event, the written materials included a copy of Arnold's own artillery orders issued only about two weeks earlier. These orders showed the exact deployment of troops in the event of a British attack. For example, Captain Daniels would send certain numbers of officers and men

---

[47] Ibid., 719.

[48] Patterson, op. cit., 123.

[49] See Lossing, op. cit., 721-23 for copies of all the materials, many in Arnold's own hand, that were turned over to André. The originals are in the New York State Library in Albany.

to each of the artillery posts along the River; Captain Thomas
would repair at once to Fort Arnold; Captain Summer's company
would remain at the north and south redoubts on the east side of
the river; Lieutenant Barber would take twenty men to
Constitution Island; and so forth. These were detailed lists of
exactly where each of more than a dozen officers would deploy all
or part of his forces. This was vital intelligence that Arnold was
handing over to André, telling him precisely where the British
should strike and in what force.

Another document, also in Arnold's hand, put the total size of
the American force at West Point and its adjacent forts as of a
week earlier at just over 3,000 men. This force was broken down
by type, size and location. Thus, at Verplanck's Point and Stony
Point, Colonel Lamb's regiment of 167 men and Colonel
Livingston's 80-man contingent made a total of 247. At North
Castle, three regiments of Connecticut militia under the command
of Colonel Wells were to be augmented by "a detachment of New
York levies of the lines" that would join "a brigade of
Massachusetts militia, and two Rank and File from New
Hampshire" for at total of nearly a thousand men, with some 852
more "on command and extra service [reserve] at Fishkill, New
Windsor, etc. who may be called in" as needed.

Other papers handed over by Arnold included charts and lists
that gave the precise numbers of men needed to man adequately
each of the forts and redoubts at West Point and vicinity, as
estimated recently by the French engineer, Villefrache: to wit, 620
at Fort Arnold, 450 at Fort Putnam, 150 at Fort Webb, 150 at
Redoubt No.1, 150 at Redoubt No. 2, 120 at North Redoubt and so
on.

Additional intelligence given to André during these early
morning hours of the September 21 included recent evaluations of
needed repairs at each fort and redoubt in a document entitled,
"Remarks on Works at West Point, a copy to be transmitted to his
Excellency, General Washington." Herein the British high
command would learn, for example, that "Fort Arnold is built of
dry fascines[50] and wood, is in a ruinous condition, incomplete, and
subject to take fire from shells," that Fort Putnam "was needing

---

[50] Bundles of sticks used to build defensive earthworks and gun batteries.

great repairs...in many places," that Fort Webb was "built of fascines and wood, a slight work, very dry, and liable to be set on fire, as the approaches are very easy, without defenses, save a slight abatis"[51] and that Redoubt No. 4 was "a wooden work about ten feet high and four or five feet thick, the west side face with a stone wall 8 feet high and four thick" but not "bomb proof" and mounting only "two six-pounders, a slight abatis" and sitting atop "a commanding piece of ground 500 yards wide."

Arnold also provided André with a bit of intelligence that would have delighted Clinton when he saw it: "The North Redoubt, on the east side, built of stone 4 feet high; above the stone, wood filled with earth, very dry, no ditch; three batteries outside the fort, a poor abatis, a rising piece of ground 500 yards to the south; the approaches under cover within 20 yards—the work easily fired with faggots[52] dipped in pitch." Arnold could hardly have been more helpful to the enemy had he offered to lead the British assault himself.

But the traitor gave even more to André on that fateful night, including the minutes of a meeting held at Washington's headquarters earlier in the month that spelled out the weaknesses of the army and revealed the gloomy prospects for improvement in its size, equipment and morale. To be certain that Clinton would have all he needed to defeat his countrymen, Arnold provided André with a detailed chart that gave the exact armaments at each fort and redoubt. Now Clinton would know how many cannon the Americans had, how many of them were howitzers and how many were mortars, as well as the number of mobile gun carriages Washington had at each of the seventeen forts, redoubts and batteries that comprised his fortifications at and near West Point.

In return for all of this vital data, André conveyed to Arnold Clinton's guarantee of £6,000 payment regardless of the outcome of the plot and £20,000 more once West Point was captured, provided that about 3,000 men and large quantities of armaments were actually surrendered there.

---

[51] A defensive obstacle made of cut trees bundled in such a way that sharpened branches pointed toward an approaching enemy.
[52] Bundles of sticks, sometimes covered with flammable material, that were used as weapons.

Arnold was not happy with the offer. He wanted an unconditional payment of £10,000 not £6,000. André assured him that he would urge the larger sum on Clinton and that his commander had promised additional rewards which were sure to please the American general. Arnold was also promised safe passage for himself and his family to New York and from there to England as well as a commission in the British Army. Events had gone too far at this point for Arnold to demur any further. He accepted the terms.

At about 4:00 a.m., after several hours of talk and with the coming of dawn, it was clear that it was time for André to get back out to *The Vulture* for his return trip to New York. But to the horror of both men, Joseph and Samuel Cohoon refused to row him out into the river, saying it was too dangerous. Nothing would persuade them. Arnold then told the reluctant André to mount one of the waiting horses and ride with him and Smith the four miles to Smith's house to spend the day before leaving for *The Vulture* after dark. André was most reluctant to disobey Clinton's order and his own good sense by traveling behind enemy lines in this manner. But he had no choice. He was now in the hands of the imposing and determined General Arnold.

As the three men, Arnold, André and Smith, made their way, riding along a plateau overlooking the river on their way to Smith's house in these early pre-dawn hours of September 22, they spied bright flashes of light coming up from the river below. It was a disturbing sight. They hurried on to Smith's house and climbed to the second story where they could have a better view. What they saw from the window overlooking the river would change everything.

Joshua Smith House: "Treason House"
Courtesy of the New-York Historical Society

Beverly Robinson House: Washington's Headquarters
Courtesy of the New-York Historical Society

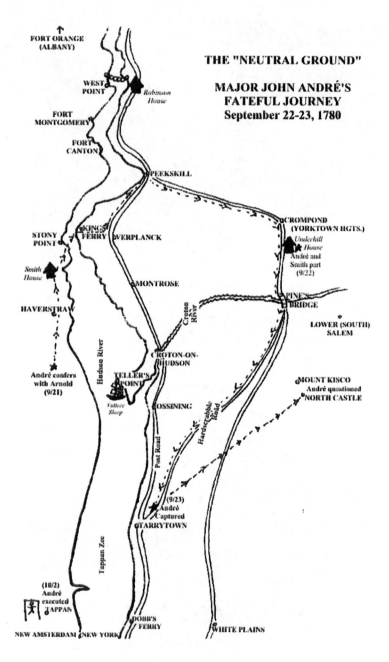

Map of the "Neutral Ground"
Drawn by Anne Secor

— CHAPTER 7 —

The Day that Changed America

What Major John André and General Benedict Arnold saw out there in the Hudson River from the second story window of Joshua Smith's house in the early hours of September 22, 1780, was the British ship *Vulture* in full retreat down river under heavy fire from pursuing American gun boats. André's escape route was disappearing before his eyes. He and Arnold now faced the daunting problem of getting him and his precious intelligence through American lines, across the dangerous neutral ground and finally safely back to Clinton in New York.

True to form, Arnold did not stay around to help his co-conspirator. After giving André all the papers that he wanted him to deliver to Clinton and telling him to hide these in his stockings, Arnold informed Joshua Smith that it was his duty to find the best way to get "Mr. Anderson" to the safety of the British lines—still not revealing to him the Englishman's real identity or mission. Arnold then gave both men a safe conduct pass, which read:

Headquarters, Robinson House
Sept. 22d, 1780

Permit Mr. John Anderson to pass the Guards to the
White Plains, or below if he chooses. He being on
public business by my direction.
B. Arnold, M. Gen.[53]

Benedict Arnold then returned to his headquarters at Colonel Robinson's house, leaving Smith and André to fend for themselves.

---

[53] Boynton, op. cit., 110.

Warily Through No Man's Land

For his part, André wanted to wait at Smith's house to see if the *The Vulture* would return to rescue him, thereby avoiding the necessity of an extensive journey overland through dangerous and unfamiliar rebel territory. Smith, on the other hand, insisted that the land route was safer. André should have no difficulty getting by American patrols using the pass that Arnold had given him. After all, as Smith saw it, "Mr. Anderson" was only a merchant from New York carrying important messages between Clinton and Arnold. But André would need to take off that British uniform. Disguising himself as a British officer in that uniform had served him well yesterday when traveling on an English ship but it would only endanger him now that he was in American territory. He would need to put on the civilian clothes that Smith provided and then follow his host through American-controlled territory and then through the neutral ground to the nearest British outpost at White Plains.

Unable to reveal his true identity, André had no choice but to follow his host's direction. He shed his uniform, put on the clothes offered by Smith and hid the incriminating documents in his boots. It was a dangerous move on André's part. Under prevailing understandings of the international rules of civilized warfare, any officer out of uniform who was caught spying behind enemy lines would not be imprisoned as an officer and gentleman and later returned in a prisoner exchange or released at the end of hostilities. He would be hanged as spy.

Late in the day of September 22, André, Smith and one of Smith's servants set out on horseback for the river crossing at nearby Kings' Ferry. A short time after crossing to the east side at Verplanck's Point, they briefly encountered Colonel Samuel Webb on the road to Peekskill. Webb knew André well but in the darkness he did not recognize his disguised fellow British officer and rode on by. A close call![54]

---

[54] For an account of André's journey toward White Plains, see Van Doren, op. cit., 337-40.

As the two traveled on toward Peekskill, they were stopped along the road by a patrol of New York militia. The officer in charge, Captain Ebenezer Boyd, was suspicious and ordered them to dismount and identify themselves. Smith complied and showed the pass from Arnold. When the captain pressed for information about what they were doing on the road at night, Smith said they were on their way to visit Major Joseph Strang. When told that Strang was not at home and it was too late to disturb his wife, Smith changed his story and said they were really intending to visit Colonel Gil Drake. Boyd suspected that Smith was lying. He knew that Drake had moved out of the state some time ago. Boyd pressed Smith for more information about his business and was told that he was the brother of the chief justice of New York, William Smith, and was on an important errand for General Arnold. He was traveling to White Plains where his companion would get vital military intelligence from a person they were to meet there.

Hearing this, Captain Boyd, probably still suspicious of the pair, decided that, in any event, it was too dangerous for them to proceed further that night. He directed them to get off the road and stay for the night at the nearby home of one Andreas Miller, just four miles from Peekskill. Here, under virtual house arrest, the two men shared a bed and, no doubt, an anxious night. Next morning by sunrise the two were up and on the road again for a few hours before stopping just south of Crompond Corners (Yorktown Heights) for breakfast at the Underhill House, a small two-story frame house set back only a few feet from the road. They dismounted at the back door and André ate his meal of mush and milk sitting on the top step at the rear of the house.

As the pair approached Pines Bridge on the Croton River early on the morning of the twenty-third, Smith abruptly informed his companion that this was as far as he would go. He would now turn back and return to Fishkill to visit his family who were staying with friends there as it was too dangerous for a well-known patriot like himself to proceed on into a region largely controlled by the British. "Mr. Anderson" would have to go on alone.

In parting, the unsuspecting Smith warned his charge not to take the westerly route because he might encounter British patrols. Rather, he should take the south road directly to White Plains.

André, of course, decided at once that the westerly road would be his best bet. Shortly after Smith departed, André crossed Pines Bridge over the Croton River and turned west toward Tarrytown on Hardscrapple Road.

He was now a solitary rider in the no man's land between the lines of the opposing forces. This, as we have seen, was where John Paulding and his fellow farmers lived and tried to eke out a living on land already abandoned by many of their former neighbors who had fled to escape the loyalist Cowboys and rebel Skinners who terrorized local farmers by scavenging for crops, livestock and other goods to sell to one army or the other. Here also, travelers were fair game for highwaymen hiding in the trees and bushes along the road waiting to rob them.

André knew as well as anyone how dangerous this area was. He had sent many of his own spies into this neutral zone to gather intelligence and carry messages to his agents among the American loyalists—duplicitous men like Colonel Beverly Robinson, and outright traitors like Benedict Arnold. Although this territory between the American post at Peekskill and the British base at White Plains was not a good place to be traveling alone, André could not help noticing, as he drew closer to Tarrytown, that some of the farms seemed to be largely intact and unspoiled by the ravages of war.

He paused by the road when a farm girl named Sally Hammond offered him a drink from the bucket of water she had just filled from a well. He rewarded her with a sixpence and rode off gratefully filled with hope that he was nearing the safety of British-held territory. A few miles later he reigned in his horse to cross a small bridge spanning Clark's Kill, a minor tributary of the Croton River.

Just a few more miles…

The Capture

Since early morning John Paulding and his two companions, David Williams and Isaac Van Wart, had been concealed in the woods alongside the road near the bridge at Clark's Kill waiting to pounce on just such a passerby as "Mr. Anderson." They were a rough and ready trio. Paulding, as we have seen, had just escaped

John André about to be captured by American militiamen. From *Harper's Weekly*, October 2, 1880, p. 629.

The Capture of John André
*Courtesy of Branch Libraries, The New York Public Library,
Astor, Lenox and Tilden Foundations*

from the notorious Bayard's Sugar Mill Prison in New York; twenty-five-year old David Williams was a four-year veteran of the New York militia who had fought in the siege of Quebec under Generals Montgomery and Arnold; twenty-one-year old Isaac Van Wart had served two years in the Westchester militia. All three were survivors of the dangerous life in the neutral ground, engaging from time to time in the raiding and looting activities of the Skinners while at the same time serving in the regular militia.

Van Wart stood guard at a fence along a wall near the road while Paulding and Williams played a game of cards nearby to pass the time. According to a later account by Williams, it was sometime between 9:00 and 10:00 a.m. when a small party of wagons and horsemen approached the bridge. Quickly recognizing them, the three allowed them to pass. But then a solitary rider approached. Van Wart alerted his companions and the three watched as the rider came into view on a small rise just above the bridge.[55]

Slowing as he came up to the bridge, André saw a large man wearing a Hessian military coat standing in the middle of the road on the other side of the bridge. The man was holding a rifle across his chest and clearly intended to block his way.

"Halt," demanded the large man, leveling his musket directly at André as his two companions joined him in the road.[56]

---

[55] For Williams's account see Boynton, op. cit., 107-109.

[56] I have dramatized the capture of André because it is, indeed, one of the most dramatic events in American history. Many other writers have done the same. I follow the lead here of John Walsh, *The Execution of Major André*, New York, 2001, 106-112. Also notable is Anthony Bailey's fictionalized biography, *Major André*, New York, 1987, 91-102; although I do not accept his characterization of the event which takes André's later account at face value. Nor do I credit the fictionalized biography of Benedict Arnold in F. J. Stimpson's, *My Story: Being the Memoir of Benedict* Arnold, New York, 1917, 567, which characterizes Paulding and his two companions as "three bushmen" and "illiterate peasants." Historians continue to disagree as to the character of the men involved in this event and as to whose memory of it to credit— Paulding's and that of his admirers or André's and that of his many sympathizers. I shall try to show that Paulding's account is more reliable.

Relieved to see the Hessian military jacket worn by the man who now took hold of his horse's reins and assuming he was finally safely within British-held territory, André replied, "I see you belong to our party."

"What party is that?" Paulding demanded.

"Why, the lower party, of course," André responded, using the familiar short-hand distinction between the British who occupied Manhattan and the lower Hudson Valley from the Americans who held most of northern Westchester County and beyond.

"Yes we do belong to the Lower Party," Paulding lied.

"Thank God," sighed André, visibly relieved and showing Paulding his expensive gold watch—the sort typically worn only by British officers.

"Please do not delay me," André continued. "I am a British officer in disguise. I have been behind American lines on important business for General Clinton and am returning to my headquarters in New York City."

Paulding realized at once that he had trapped a prize. "Get down," he ordered, brandishing his rifle at André. "We are not of the lower party. We are Americans."

"I must warn you. You are interfering with the business of the Crown" was the reply from a shaken André.

"Get down from that horse and identify yourself."

Dismounting nervously, André changed his story completely. "I am not really a British officer. I said that only because I thought you were loyalists and would not let a patriot pass. I am also an American. My name is John Anderson. I am on an errand for General Arnold at West Point."

The three men examined the safe-conduct pass to White Plains that André now tendered. Paulding's native instincts were aroused. He was suspicious. Something about this "John Anderson" and his nervous laugh did not seem genuine. The man had seemed more believable in his initial claim to be a British officer.

André made a move to remount. "Not yet," Paulding commanded. "Please come with us over here among the trees. We need to search you."

André's voice became stern and authoritative as he looked each of the three in the eye and said, "Look here, you men,

General Arnold has sent me to meet an agent at Dobbs Ferry. You will be in serious trouble if you don't let me pass."

At this, Paulding nodded to the other two and they each took André firmly by an arm and led him back into the woods.

"Just a little search, just to be sure," Paulding said to André. "Now turn out your pockets, please. Now take off your coat! Your vest! Your jacket!"

The men searched all of these carefully but found nothing incriminating and little of value beyond the expensive gold watch.

"Now the boots."

André sat down on a rock and Williams pulled off his left boot while Van Wart removed the right one. "Nothing," they reported to their leader. "Take off your stockings," Paulding ordered his captive.

"Something here in this one," shouted Van Wart as he pulled off André's knee-length hose and held up a package of papers that had been concealed there.

"More papers here," barked Williams, as he produced a similar package from beneath André's other stocking.

Paulding, the only one of the three Americans who could read, quickly perused the six sheets of closely written material. Then he compared the signature at the end of each page with that on André's pass from Arnold. They seemed to be in the same hand.

"These papers contain detailed information about West Point, the numbers and location of men and guns. Each of them seems to be signed by General Arnold. Where did you get these?" he demanded.

"From a man I met at Pine's Bridge. I am supposed to deliver them to another man at Dobbs's Ferry. That's all I know."

"This pass from Arnold is a forgery, isn't it?" demanded Paulding, still not willing to accept that Arnold might be a traitor.

"No, it isn't," answered André truthfully.

Paulding pondered the situation a final time and then made his decision.

"This man is a spy," he declared to his companions. "We will deliver him to Colonel Jameson at North Point and let him sort this out."

"You are making a mistake, gentlemen. I am not a spy. I am an agent of General Arnold, delivering and receiving vital information on his behalf," the English spy asserted with ironic truthfulness.

"As soon as he is dressed, bind his arms securely and get him on his horse," Paulding directed his comrades.

Desperate now, André tried a new tack: bribery. "I can't explain this to you. But if you let me go I will see that you receive a large reward. In the meantime, take my gold watch."[57]

"How big a reward?" Williams demanded. "A hundred guineas?

"Just let me go," entreated André, "and when I get to my destination I will send a reward not of 100 but 1,000 guineas to any place that you designate. You can have my horse, also. I will leave it for you at Dobbs Ferry."

Sensing from their expressions that the men were too wise—or too wily—to trust him to send the money once they let him go, André tried a final offer. "Just hold me here and I will give one of you a note to take to a person who will give you the money. I will trust you to release me after you have been paid."

Now Paulding realized for certain that his captive was a British spy. André would not be offering such a reward if he were truly on an errand for General Arnold. Paulding decided that he would confirm his suspicions by taking the Englishman for questioning to the nearest military outpost which was only a short distance away at North Castle, near Mount Kisco.

Along the twelve-mile ride with their captive on the road northward, Van Wart noticed that André had begun to sweat profusely. "Only a few moments before," Van Wart later reported, the prisoner "was uncommonly gay in his looks, but after we made him a prisoner you could read his face that he thought it was all over with him." When taunted by Williams with the question of

---

[57] André would later claim that the men were common thieves who had tried to bribe him, not the other way around. Many believed his version of the story, especially as he succeeded later in rousing enormous sympathy for himself. In later sworn statements at André's trial in 1780 and in 1817 during his later request for a pension renewal, Paulding admitted that the trio had taken André's watch and also his horse, saddle and bridle as "prizes" of war and later sold them and divided the money. Walsh, op. cit., 166.

whether he would try to escape if they gave him the opportunity, André said that he would. Then he added, "I wish to God you had blown my brains out when you stopped me!"

Just south of Mount Kisco, the four men reached Mile Square, an outpost at North Castle. Here a dragoon of soldiers was stationed under the temporary command of twenty-eight-year old Lieutenant Colonel John Jameson. The colonel, like other commanders in the area, had been told that if a "Mr. Anderson" was brought to him for any reason he should be delivered at once to General Arnold at West Point. (This was Arnold's fail-safe strategy in the event that André was captured behind American lines.)

When John Paulding handed over to Colonel Jameson the papers that "Mr. Anderson" had hidden in his boot, the Colonel was immediately suspicious. He dispatched the documents, along with a description of the conditions of his prisoner's capture, to George Washington, who was at the time en route southward from his meetings with the French at Hartford. The commander in chief had been expected to travel to his headquarters at Peekskill by way of New Salem but had taken a different more northern route instead, traveling by way of Fishkill. In the event, Jameson's messenger took much longer than had been anticipated to reach Washington, finding him at Danbury, Connecticut late Sunday, the twenty-fourth.[58]

By the time Washington had any idea of what had happened at Tarrytown, frantic confusion would grip the lives of all of the major participants in this fateful drama, except for John Paulding. Washington, André, Arnold, Peggy Shippen Arnold, Sir Henry Clinton and several others who were to play subordinate but significant roles would all be caught up in a tangled web of deceit, revenge and fear from which none of them would fully escape.

---

[58] Van Doren, op. cit., 341 ff. provides a thorough account of what happened to André after his capture at Tarrytown. See also Walsh, op. cit., 115, ff.

CHAPTER 8

A Tangled Web

Once again, John André nearly escaped. Colonel Jameson had acted wisely and quickly by sending the critical intelligence about an apparent plot to George Washington rather than to Benedict Arnold. But, for some reason, although he obviously suspected that "Mr. Anderson" was a spy or at least a double agent, he did not hold his captive in custody. Nor did he send him to Washington. Inexplicably, he sent him under guard and on foot to General Arnold at West Point and, at the same time, sent a message on ahead of the prisoner by speedy courier to alert Arnold to the prisoner's arrival.

For what reason, other than incompetence, would Jameson, on the one hand, so strongly suspect that Arnold was a traitor that he would send evidence to that effect to Washington and yet, on the other hand, blindly obey a standing order from Arnold that if "Mr. Anderson" were ever brought in he should send him directly to Arnold? Why didn't Jameson send both the incriminating papers and the captive either to Arnold or Washington?

One explanation for such a seemingly foolish action is that Jameson was not competent to be in charge of an important military outpost.[59] He held the command only temporarily while the senior officer, Colonel Elisha Sheldon, was relieved of his duties while being tried by a military court for a variety of offenses. On the other hand, perhaps Jameson was no fool at all but a loyal and obedient officer who, like many in the subordinate ranks of the colonial army, deeply admired Benedict Arnold.

---

[59] One commentator has gone so far as to describe Jameson's actions as "stupid." R. Brown, "Three Forgotten Heroes," *American Heritage Magazine*, May, 1957, 27.

Perhaps this whole affair of "Mr. Anderson" and his incriminating papers was an elaborate hoax, a British plot, to discredit Arnold. How was Jameson to know? Best to cover his bets and give part of what he had (the papers) to Washington and the other part (the alleged spy) to Arnold. Let them sort it out.

What to Do with "Mr. Anderson"

In the event, Jameson ordered Lieutenant Solomon Allen to take six troopers and escort "Mr. Anderson" to Arnold at West Point. He gave Allen a letter for Arnold.

> I have sent Lieutenant Allen with a certain John Anderson taken [while] going into New York. He had a pass signed with your name. He had a parcel of papers taken from under his stockings, which I think of a very dangerous tendency.
>
> The papers I have sent to George Washington. They contain the number of cannon, etc., the different pieces of ground that command each fort, and what distance they are from the different forts; the situation of each fort, and what may be set on fire with bombs and carcasses, and what are out of repair; the speech of General Washington to the Council of War held the sixth of this month; the situation of our armies in general...[60]

By early evening, Lieutenant Allen and his patrol were on the road with their securely bound captive. By shortly after midnight they should arrive at Arnold's headquarters along the Hudson. Of course, as soon as Arnold saw André and read this letter, he would know that his plans were foiled and he would flee for his life.

While André, no doubt quietly rejoicing at his good fortune and buoyed by renewed hope of escape, was proceeding under guard along the road toward Arnold's headquarters at Robinson House, an event that would destroy his last chance of freedom was afoot back at North Castle. Major Benjamin Tallmadge, a ranking officer at the post who had been away for a short time, returned about an hour after André left. Tallmadge was an experienced

---

[60] Walsh, op. cit., 116.

intelligence officer who had previously encountered suspicious information about a "Mr. Anderson." As soon as he was informed of what had happened and was told the contents of Jameson's letter to Arnold, he realized what was going on between the spy and the traitor and urged Jameson to send out a party at once to bring André back to North Castle. At first, Jameson refused. There was no way that the courageous patriot, Benedict Arnold, could be a traitor. It was unthinkable.

As Tallmadge considered the matter further, he became convinced that immediate action was necessary to prevent Arnold from carrying out a plot to wreck the Revolution. He demanded that Jameson authorize him to take a full troop of soldiers to West Point immediately to arrest Arnold and control the situation until Washington could get there to take control. There might well follow a battle with troops loyal to Arnold who were probably already readying the base for surrender to the British. There was no time to lose.

Jameson was appalled. He would give no such order. Under constant pressure from Tallmadge, he relented somewhat. He would send out a patrol to bring the captive back. Once again, however, the cagey colonel hedged his bets. He ordered that, although "Mr. Anderson" should be returned, his letter to Arnold must be carried on to the general. Jameson was taking no chances of losing his reputation as a patriot should Arnold turn out to be a hero and not a traitor after all. He gave the officer sent to retrieve the prisoner a note for Lieutenant Allen:

Sir,

For some circumstances I have just heard, I have reason to fear that a party of the enemy are above; and as I would not have Anderson retaken or get away, I desire that you would proceed to Lower Salem with him and deliver him to Captain Hoogland. You will leave the guard with Captain Hoogland also, except one man whom you may take along. You may proceed on to West Point and deliver the letter to General Arnold. You may also show him this, that he may know the reason why the prisoner is not sent on. You will please to return as soon as you can to your business.[61]

As the messenger raced through the night to intercept Allen and his prisoner –on a ride that one historian has said rivaled that of Paul Revere in historic importance—he estimated that at a full gallop he could overtake Lieutenant Allen, who had left two hours before but would be traveling at a slower pace, somewhere near Peekskill, just short of the Hudson River.[62] It would be a close call. Once at the riverside house of Colonel Robinson, the captive would be safely in the protection of General Arnold.

Riding at breakneck speed, the rider reached the outskirts of Peekskill but failed to see Allen and his party of eight soldiers anywhere. Fearful that he had missed his quarry, he rode frantically through the streets of Peekskill in search of them. Finally, he spotted the small band just beyond St. Peter's Church on the northern edge of the town. When Lieutenant Allen spied the messenger's panting horse, he later recalled that he was looking at an animal that was "bloody with spurring, and fire-red with haste."

One can imagine André's horror at this moment. So close to escape, his major fear had been that Arnold had already fled and their plot been exposed before he could arrive at Arnold's headquarters. Now he heard that he was to be returned to a post located well inside American lines at Lower (South) Salem, some fifteen miles northeast of North Castle near the Connecticut border.

When Lieutenant Allen arrived at South Salem with his captive early in the morning of the twenty-fourth, he turned André over to the officer of the day, Lieutenant Joshua King, who later recalled that André "looked somewhat like a reduced gentleman," wearing "handsome white-topped boots," a "somewhat threadbare" purple coat "trimmed with gold lace," and "a small beaver [cap] on his head." No doubt André did look something the worse for wear after the harrowing experiences of the past day. But exhausted, discouraged and disheveled as he was, the ever-

---

[61] Ibid., 121.
[62] A dramatic and well-documented account of this historic ride is Walsh, op. cit, 115-122.

resourceful Englishman set about on a new tack to gain his freedom.[63]

How Can Such a Man be a Spy?

Locked in a room, André at once began to ingratiate himself with the American officers, including Lieutenant King, who stayed there with him much of the time, and Major Tallmadge, who had ridden up from North Castle to question the prisoner. Ever the charming, winsome gentlemen, André managed to convince several of the Americans that he was no villain at all but a victim of circumstances. Even Tallmadge, who now had his original suspicions about the prisoner confirmed and wished he had acted on his own to stop the plot and arrest Arnold, was impressed that here was

> an officer of breeding, a charming gentleman who was pleasant to converse with even under these circumstances.

As soon as André was secured in his room, he asked Lieutenant King if he might have his clothes washed. King not only granted this request but had a barber brought in to shave André and wash his hair. King noted later that there was powder in André's hair. Surely this was no ordinary man but a person of some distinction. Could he really be a spy? Or was he, as he claimed, a distinguished British officer on an important mission from General Clinton to General Arnold. Or, at the least, was he not probably a British officer captured behind enemy lines and eligible for some future prisoner exchange? He certainly did not seem to be the run-of-the-mill spy often seen and sometimes captured in the neutral zone. He was, after all, one of us: an officer and a gentleman.

André's request for pen and paper to write a letter to General Washington was granted immediately. In the letter he told Washington what he had told King, Tallmadge and other officers at South Salem: he was a British officer named John André. He was an English gentleman. He was not really concerned about his safety, either while on his mission or now while in captivity. His

---

[63] Ibid., 123.

only concern was his honor. He did not want it tarnished by the idea that he had "assumed a mean character for treacherous purposes of self-interest, a conduct incompatible with principles that actuated me, as well as with my condition in life."

He admitted to Washington that he was indeed on a mission from General Clinton designed to secure valuable intelligence from an American source. (He never mentioned Arnold my name.) He told Washington that he had remained in uniform as a British officer until forced against his will by his treacherous and traitorous American colleagues to shed his uniform, to assume a disguise and to travel behind American lines. None of this had been his original intent; but what else was he to do under the circumstances? He was only "involuntarily an imposter." Was not an officer permitted to employ extreme measures to save his life and maintain his stature as a gentleman?[64]

As if this defense were not already so implausible as to be insulting, André went further in his message to Washington and betrayed his total arrogance and disrespect for even for the highest ranking American. The thirty-year-old second-level enemy officer now threatened George Washington with retribution if he did not release him. If his petition were not granted, there would be retaliation against American prisoners held by the British in South Carolina. In closing, André, who never denied that he was in fact on a mission that if successful could have cost Washington his life and America her independence—a fact apparently irrelevant in this circumstance—addressed Washington as an equal, one who like him was, after all, of "superior station."[65]

Although Washington would not for a moment be taken in by André's intemperate and self-serving letter when he received it several days later, some of his guards at South Salem and later at Tappan were more sympathetic. How did André manage to convince them to see his side of the story? He did so by appealing in so charming a manner to their natural affinity for a fellow officer, especially one who embodied so many of the gentlemanly qualities they admired and sought to emulate. Class snobbery trumped patriotic feeling. André was admired as an officer who

---

[64] Van Doren, op. cit, 342.
[65] Walsh, op. cit., 125-6.

managed, under the most trying circumstances imaginable, to retain his dignity and composure and not in any way seek to denigrate the officers who held him in captivity. Spies could not be cultivated gentlemen. Beyond that, they found André's account of what had happened to him along the road after he had left General Arnold at West Point more plausible than the story told by his captors, John Paulding and his two companions.

For example, André told Isaac Bronson, the doctor at South Salem who came to check him over, that his captors were nothing but ruffians who were trying to rob him. They threw him to the ground, ripped open his clothes, tore off his boots and then tried to extort money from him as the price for his release. This failing, they took all that he had of value—his horse and his gold watch—and then turned him in at North Castle, not out of patriotism but in hopes of reward for capturing so prominent an officer. Perhaps, too, the officers were more inclined to disbelieve the stories of the local farmers and ruffians who made up their militia and were numbered among the destructive raiders during this chaotic time. This was a theme that André would expand at his trial a few days later.

Once his letter to Washington was on its way, André seemed to relax. He made a whimsical drawing of himself in the company of his captors and then settled into his bunk for a nap. It had been a long two days since his departure from *The Vulture* to meet General Arnold.

Meanwhile Up and Down the Hudson

While André was penning his letter to George Washington from Lower Salem on September 24, the American commander-in-chief was still unaware of the momentous events that had occurred in the past two days: Arnold's betrayal and André's flight, capture and imprisonment. Washington was, at the time, on his way from his meeting with the French officers at Hartford to his base at Tappan on the Hudson, by way of a brief stop en route for a scheduled breakfast meeting with Benedict Arnold at West Point. Traveling with him were Generals the Marquis de Lafayette and Henry Knox. Realizing that he might be late for breakfast, he dispatched his aide, twenty-three-year-old Colonel Alexander

Hamilton on ahead with the luggage and an apology to Mrs. Arnold for their slight delay. He also sent Majors James McHenry and Samuel Shaw, aides to Lafayette and Knox respectively, to represent these two generals.

Similarly, Benedict Arnold had no idea of what was happening while he awaited word of the timing of the British attack. He had no inkling that André had been captured and his plot exposed. He and Peggy were at Robinson House anticipating Washington's arrival. With luck he would be able to deliver the forts and Washington to the British with one stroke.

As for General Clinton, he was still waiting in New York for the overdue André carrying the plans to West Point that would make his attack on West Point a certain success. None of the principals in the drama had any idea that their plans, their lives and the course of history had already been dramatically altered.

Meanwhile breakfast had begun at Arnold's headquarters at Robinson House. Arnold, his long-time aide, Major David Franks, Washington's emissary, Alexander Hamilton and the other officers were still eating when Arnold was summoned by an aide to the buttery. There he was confronted by a road-weary Lieutenant Allen, just arrived with the fateful letter from Colonel Jameson. One can imagine the emotions that coursed through Arnold's whole being as he read that letter. His entire life was changed in an instant. There would be no glory, fame and wealth for him now. He was an exposed traitor. He must flee at once. How would Clinton and the British receive him? Washington would be here at any moment. What, if anything, did he know?

No doubt maintaining the outward composure of a man with impressive military bearing, Arnold told Lieutenant Allen to wait for a reply. But inwardly he must have been scheming at top speed. He then went outside and ordered that his horse be saddled and a barge readied immediately for a trip across the river. Then he hobbled inside the house and upstairs to his wife. Peggy was resting comfortably in bed, still pleasantly warmed by all the attention that Washington's young officers had been lavishing upon her. (The commander-in-chief liked to joke that half the men on his staff were in love with her.)

"All is lost," Arnold told his wife. At that moment there was a knock on their bedroom door. The voice outside belonged to the ever-faithful Major Franks, who announced that Washington's party was approaching and would be there momentarily. It was time to come downstairs and greet the commander-in-chief.

Arnold jumped up from the edge of the bed and rushed out the door, downstairs and out of the house, almost knocking Franks down as he hobbled past his aide in unseemly haste. He had to hurry across the river to West Point to prepare a suitable reception for Washington, he shouted back to his aides and guests, never looking back. The traitor mounted his horse and took off at a gallop for the river's edge. Almost immediately, he encountered an advance party of Washington's entourage. Recovering his composure after an instant of panic, he told the men to stable their horses in the barn. Then he resumed his gallop toward the river, no doubt leaving the soldiers wondering where their host was going in such haste. Before they could react, he was gone. Once at the wharf Arnold ordered the boatman to take him across the river to Stony Point.

Danger had not yet passed. Just as Arnold's barge was leaving the dock, a boat from West Point came toward the wharf and the officers aboard saw him. They must surely have wondered: Why in the world would Arnold be leaving just as Washington was arriving? He hollered across the short span of water separating the two barges that they should go on up to the house and tell Washington that he would be back by supper-time. They seemed to accept this for the moment. In the middle of the river, Arnold announced to the bargemen that he was not going to West Point at all but was on a special mission for Washington to the captain of the British sloop *The Vulture* anchored down river off Teller's Point near Sing Sing. He promised the somewhat suspicious crew that they would have two gallons of rum for the inconvenience of this immediate change of course and they complied.

Ever since André had left *The Vulture* four days earlier to meet Benedict Arnold, the ship's commander, Captain Sutherland, and his important passenger, the British loyalist, Colonel Beverly Robinson, had been waiting impatiently for "Anderson's" return. They had been driven from their anchorage off Teller's Point by rebel gun boats on Friday night but returned soon after to keep their vigil. On the third day of their wait, Sunday, the 24th, Robinson sent a note off to Clinton in New York reporting that as yet nothing had been seen or heard of "John Anderson," and he feared that something most have gone wrong on shore.

At about mid-day on September 25, Sutherland and Robinson spotted General Arnold's barge heading toward them from upriver. They assumed that at long last André was returning and they could leave for New York and be a part of the successful campaign to take West Point and secure the Hudson. When Arnold came aboard and told them his story they were deeply disturbed. All had failed. Arnold had failed. Worst of all, he had forced their "Mr. Anderson" to flee by land through enemy territory while he, the traitor, was taking the safe escape route down river on *The Vulture*.

As for the traitor, he may have hoped for the reception of a hero who was unsuccessful in his attempt to hand over West Point but was nevertheless still able to be of great service as an able British general and an example to other prospective deserters. But his initial reception did not portend such.

That Arnold would not be an example to fellow Americans was immediately evident when he told the nine crewmen who had carried him from his headquarters of his defection and urged them to join him. When they refused to a man, he angrily ordered that Captain Sutherland put them in irons as prisoners of war.

Before the sloop departed for New York, Arnold sent off a message to George Washington. It was one of the most audacious and paranoid letters he had ever written, redeemed only by the admirable, if desperate, motive to help his wife. "I have ever acted from a principle of love to my country," he began. He continued that there was no point in his trying to defend himself from those to whom his actions "may appear inconsistent" with his words. After all, such people "seldom judge right of any man's actions." He had too "often experienced the ingratitude of my country" to expect any favors now he said to the man who had stood by him throughout his troubled and checkered career. But would the general be so kind as to see that his wife, who was a true innocent, be delivered safely either to him in New York or her family in Philadelphia?[66]

---

[66] Van Doren, op. cit., 348-9.

A Commander Betrayed

Colonel Robinson also sent a letter to Washington with the same courier. His purpose was to defend André who he had just learned from Arnold was in captivity and would probably be tried as a spy. Robinson wanted Washington to know that André had come ashore in his uniform under a flag of truce on a mission from General Clinton to General Arnold. He had later only been obeying Arnold, the American commander in the area, in everything he did: abandon the flag of truce, change clothing and hide papers on his person that had been given him by Arnold. Under the circumstances, Washington should immediately release André. To do otherwise would be to ignore rules of civilized warfare.[67]

George Washington, in company of Lafayette, Knox and members of his staff arrived at Robinson House just moments before Arnold's hasty departure. He was surprised to find neither Arnold nor his wife there to greet him. Mrs. Arnold was ill and upstairs in bed, he was told by Major Franks. As for the general, he had gone across to West Point to prepare a proper reception for the commander-in-chief. This all seemed plausible enough. After breakfast, Washington, leaving Hamilton behind at the Robinson House, crossed the river with Lafayette and Knox in expectation of a welcoming cannon salute to be followed by a fine reception within the fort. Nothing of the sort occurred. In fact, once inside the headquarters at West Point, Washington was informed by Arnold's embarrassed aide, Colonel David Lamb, that he was not expecting his general at all that day.

We don't need to imagine how miffed the protocol-conscious Washington was to be stood up in this way. He tells us his reaction

---

[67] It would always be a matter of controversy whether André had come ashore under a flag of truce. If so, he would clearly not be guilty of spying under the prevailing laws of warfare. Robinson's letter was offered into evidence at André's trial, but the flag of truce contention was refuted by his accusers. Ibid., 357-8. A distinguished contemporary loyalist historian, who had served as a justice of the New York Supreme Court, insisted that André and Robinson had come "under the sanction of a flag." Thomas Jones, *History of New York During the Revolution*, New York (1787), 1879, 370.

in his diary: "The impropriety of his conduct when he knew I was to be there, struck me very forcibly and my mind misgave me; but I had not the least idea of the real cause."[68] He soon would know it all. Before re-crossing the river to Robinson House, Washington, beginning to suspect that an attack at West Point might be imminent, made a quick inspection of the fortifications and, to his horror, found them to be in terrible repair and disturbingly inadequate to withstand any serious assault.

Meanwhile, the message that Colonel Jameson had sent to Washington from North Castle two days before, along with the papers discovered on André's person, finally arrived at Robinson House. In Washington's absence, Alexander Hamilton read the letter and examined the incriminating papers. Scarcely had he digested the message and its implications when Washington and his party returned from West Point. Hamilton immediately handed the material to his commander.

The ever-trusting Washington was horrified by what he read. There was no doubt now that Arnold had totally betrayed him and was the worst traitor imaginable. With remarkable composure, Washington dispatched Hamilton and McHenry at once to capture Arnold. They set out with all haste down the Post Road toward Verplanck's Point to intercept the fugitive. It was too late. By then, Arnold was already far down river, safely aboard *The Vulture*. He had written his letter to Washington and was on his way to New York. By the time the two men reached Verplanck's Point, Arnold's letter to Washington was there waiting for them. They picked it up and returned to the Robinson house.

"Arnold has betrayed us. Whom can we trust now?" Washington, in a state of some despair, exclaimed to Lafayette shortly after dispatching his aides to capture Arnold. This was only a temporary outburst. In short order, the commander-in-chief was in control again, sitting down to a mid-day dinner with Lafayette, Knox and their aides to discuss what was to be done beyond waiting to hear if Arnold had been captured.

---

[68] Wallace, op. cit., 251.

Fights and Fits in a Traitor's House

Washington questioned Arnold's aides, Colonel Richard Varick and Major David Franks, to discover what they knew about the traitor's plans. He may already have suspected that these two quarrelsome officers knew more than they were telling. What he did not know is that morale among Arnold's staff at Robinson House had deteriorated badly in recent days, especially in the relationship between Varick and Franks on the one hand, and Arnold's friend and helpmate in the André affair, Joshua Hett Smith.

Varick and Franks had grown jealous and suspicious of Smith. They managed to convince Peggy Arnold that she should share their attitudes toward the lawyer from the distinguished Smith family of New York who had recently developed such a close and confidential relationship with her husband. Varick was especially vindictive, going so far as to speak openly against Smith to Arnold himself and to threaten that if his commander did not immediately end his close relationship with Smith he would leave Robinson House for a new assignment. This little cabal of Varick, Franks and Peggy Arnold was in no mood to welcome Smith when he arrived on the twenty-fourth to report to Arnold—out of their hearing—on his success in getting André into the neutral zone and almost to British-held White Plains.[69]

Exasperated, the two aides proceeded to pick a fight with Smith that very day during lunch. At issue was the weighty matter of whether the cost of salt should be accounted in American dollars or, as Smith said, in English pence. So insulting were Varick and Franks to Smith that Arnold became angry with them both. After Smith left to travel home to Haverstraw, Franks attacked him behind his back again. This time Arnold had had enough and instructed his aide to hold his tongue. At this, Franks

---

[69] Franks was a Jewish merchant from Montreal who joined Arnold's forces during the invasion of Canada earlier in the War. He had been a member of Arnold's staff for two years. Varick was an officer in a New York regiment and had been an aide to General Philip Schuyler who commanded the northern army. He had been on Arnold's staff for only a few weeks. Both men found Arnold temperamental and difficult to work for. Koke, op. cit., 65-66.

stormed out of the house saying that he wished to leave Arnold's staff. Varick tried to calm Arnold but continued to insist that Smith was an unworthy confidant for the general, showing him a letter to that effect that he had received recently from Governor Clinton's office. Wishing, no doubt, to deflect suspicion of his recent activities with Smith, Arnold agreed to end the relationship.[70]

Such, then, was the frame of mind of Varick and Franks as Washington began to question them about the Arnolds. Varick, who was ill with a fever at the time, was nevertheless able to tell Washington a strange tale about Peggy Arnold's behavior. It seems that while lying in his bed the day before, just after Washington and his party had left the house for West Point, he heard a shriek from Peggy's room upstairs. As he ran toward the stairs, she was on her way down to his room in her night dress, hair disheveled, screaming hysterically. She grabbed hold of him and cried out, "Colonel Varick, did you order my child to be killed?" Then, according to Varick, the distraught woman knelt down in front of him and begged him not to kill her baby. Franks heard the commotion and rushed in to calm Peggy.

The resident doctor, William Eustis, was summoned and the three men managed to get Peggy back into bed. She was composed for a short time before crying out in despair that she had no friends at all in this place. Varick assured her that he and Franks were her friends and that her husband would be home again soon. "No," she shrieked. "General Arnold will never return. He is gone, He is gone forever, *there, there, there*, the spirits have carried him up there; they have put hot irons on his head," she said, pointing to the ceiling.[71]

Shortly after Washington returned to Robinson House from his trip across river to West Point, Peggy Arnold became so distraught that Eustice, Varick and Franks decided Washington should be summoned upstairs to try to calm her. By now the three men may have begun to suspect the true reason for Arnold's hasty departure and to assume that the cause of Peggy's distress was that

---

[70] Richard Koke, *Accomplice to Treason: Joshua Hett Smith and the Arnold Conspiracy*, New York, 1973, 99-102.
[71] Van Doren, op. cit., 346-8.

her husband had told her before he left that his plot had been uncovered and that he was fleeing for his life. If they had any such suspicion, they did not reveal it to Washington. He could form his own opinion about her hysteria.

When Washington entered Peggy's room, she was screaming that a hot iron was on her head and only Washington could remove it. When Varick told her that Washington was here to help her, she clutched her infant son to her breast, screaming, "No! That is not General Washington! That is the man who is going to assist Colonel Varick in killing my child." The austere commander, who had known Peggy since she was a child, tried to comfort the lady with news that, although her husband's plot had been discovered, he had escaped. Unable to console her, Washington went back downstairs, quite unaware that Peggy Arnold had been completely implicated in—and may even have instigated—the entire betrayal more than a year before.

Nor was Washington the only one who was certain of her innocence.

About this time, Hamilton returned from Verplanck's Point. When he visited Peggy in her room, he found her alternately calm and hysterical but in every way a sympathetic young woman.

> One moment she raved, another she melted into tears. Sometimes she pressed her infant to her bosom and lamented its fate occasioned by the imprudence of its father, in a manner that would have penetrated insensibility itself.[72]

Some hours later, Hamilton visited Peggy again, this time in company of other similarly smitten young officers, and "sought to soothe her by every method in my power..."

> She received us in bed, with every circumstance that would interest our sympathy, and her sufferings were so eloquent that I wished myself her brother to have a right to enable me to give her proofs of my friendship.[73]

Alexander Hamilton and the other men at Robinson House, including the courtly commander-in-chief, could not do enough to

---

[72] Flexner, op. cit., 374.
[73] Ibid.

soothe the lovely twenty-year-old Peggy Shippen Arnold. They
hovered around her bed, brought her flowers, talked sweetly to
her. The irresistible charms of the Philadelphia femme fatale were
once again at full float. All of these men were, as Washington had
said, to one degree or another in love with her.

What Will Become of Peggy?

As they made preparations to escort the distressed young woman
safely out of harm's way, the men at Robinson House urged Peggy
not to return to New York to be with her husband. He was a
scoundrel who was unworthy of her loyalty, much less her warm
and delicate affections. She should instead return to her family in
Philadelphia where she would be properly nurtured and cared for
in a manner suitable to her sensitive nature. Peggy did not argue.
Although she had been complicit in the treason from the beginning
and had dreamed of great wealth and prestige as her husband rose
to prominence in British America, she had no wish to share his
fate as a man who would be forever hated by one-half of the
population, perhaps not trusted by the other and likely forced to
flee into exile. No, thank you. Peggy would return to her family in
Philadelphia, to the comfortable and secure status of a grieving but
still beautiful and charming young woman of good breeding and
perhaps, someday, with a future with another man of good
promise.

And so Peggy set out for Philadelphia under the protection of
Major Franks, the most faithful of her sycophants among the
officers at Robinson House. She was not well received along the
road because, by this time, word of her husband's treason had
spread. When they reached Paramus, New Jersey, they spent the
night with her old friend, the loyalist widow, Theodosia Prevost.
At last in the company of a woman she could trust with her awful
secret and who would praise her for what she had done, Peggy
poured out the whole painful tale of her role in the failed plan to
defeat the rebels and of the ridiculous charade she had been forced

to play for several days in order to hide her deeds from Washington and his officers.[74]

Back in Philadelphia, less than a week after her husband's flight from Robinson House, Peggy was soon the unwilling center of growing controversy about what her husband had done and her role in his deeds. Her father, Edward, staunchly defended her innocence and insisted that she was really just a young girl who had been taken advantage of by this terrible traitor. Edward was supported in his defense of her by such notables as John Jay and Robert Morris. Others in the city, including the powerful Ruling Council, were not so sure.

When a letter that André had written to Peggy a year before the treason surfaced and was published, there were claims that this was probably but one of many letters between the two conspirators, with Peggy playing—as indeed she had—a key role in the relationship between André and Arnold. There were demands that Peggy be forced out of the city and required to join her husband with the British in New York.

As for the lady herself, she retreated to her bedroom and was alternately inclined, amidst much weeping and other signs of melancholy, to deny her involvement in her husband's actions and to express the desire to be with him again. While her father used all of his prestige and influence to protect her, she sometimes seemed unwilling to support his condemnations of her husband and his insistence that she had never shared any of his British sympathies.

Meanwhile, Benedict Arnold was in New York, safe from those he had betrayed but failing to receive anything like the welcome he had hoped for. He needed and wanted the sympathy and comfort of his beautiful young wife. Where was she? Had Washington discovered her role in the plot and failed to release her? Had she chosen to return to her father rather than come to him?

---

[74] Theodosia Prevost later married Aaron Burr and told him of Peggy Arnold's confession. That gentleman kept the secret until both Arnolds were dead. As this is the only reported admission by Peggy, she was able to keep up her pretense of innocence for the rest of her long life.

Major characters in the drama. Top: Maj. Tallmadge.
Middle, left to right: Col. B. Robinson, Gen. Arnold, Maj. André.
Bottom: John Paulding.
Courtesy of Branch Libraries, The New York Public Library,
Astor, Lenox and Tilden Foundations

John André: A self-sketch on the eve of his execution
Courtesy of the Yale University Art Gallery

André's death warrant presented
Courtesy of the New-York Historical Society

CHAPTER 9

Trial and Execution

George Washington did not spend much time worrying about Mrs. Arnold or fretting over the enormity of her husband's betrayal. The commander-in-chief was busy at once making preparations to defend West Point and other fortifications along the river from what he feared was an imminent British attack. He had to assume that Clinton had received Arnold's information and was already on his way upriver. He ordered the ranking officers at West Point to prepare at once for an attack. He sent a message to General Greene at Tappan ordering him to bring a large part of the army stationed there up to King's Ferry with all speed. He relieved the prickly Colonel James Livingston, whom he wrongly suspected of complicity with Arnold, of his command at Tellers Point.

Even as Washington worked to make the best of a bad situation, he considered the possible consequences of Arnold's treason for the future of the young country. Had the traitor acted alone? Who might he have recruited to defect with him? Was the garrison at West Point still loyal?

As for the immediate question of what to do with Major John André, Washington had by this time received André's insulting letter from Lower Salem protesting innocence. He had also received Beverly Robinson's message from *The Vulture* with a somewhat different rendition of the facts of the case but a similar assertion of André's innocence. His reaction to Robinson's letter was to send a message to Lieutenant King at South Salem ordering him to keep André under especially close guard and in no way to regard him as an ordinary prisoner of war. As for André's letter, he considered it unworthy of response. Unlike many of his junior officers, he was not under the spell of the charming young Englishman.

So far as Washington was concerned, when André had taken off his uniform, donned a disguise and moved behind American lines, he had become a spy. A military person, especially an officer, who was captured in enemy territory was a combatant and entitled to certain protections under civilized rules of warfare. These included humane treatment and release after the end of hostilities or through prisoner exchanges during the war. A spy, on the other hand, was the lowest order of combatant: a scoundrel, a sneak. He might be either a civilian or a soldier in disguise. If caught during wartime, he could expect to be summarily tried and executed.

Without hesitation, Washington ordered that André be held securely at Lower Salem until a military court of inquiry could be convened at which time he should be brought under heavy guard to West Point and then to the place of his trial and, so far as Washington was concerned, his certain execution by hanging. The trial would be held at army headquarters at Tappan, a small village on the west side of the Hudson near the New Jersey border.

An Officer, a Gentleman and a Spy

André was brought under heavy guard from Lower Salem to West Point and then down river to Tappan. Here he was imprisoned in the Mabie Tavern, a long, low stone building that served as headquarters for General Nathaniel Greene, the area commander. He was held in two small rooms adjoining the sitting room that extended across the front of the house. On the other side of the sitting room was a large area that served as the commander's office. As Greene led André to his quarters, he later remembered thinking that he had been, under the circumstances, surprised by the prisoner's "apparent cheerfulness." Surely he must know that his life was now measured in days.

General Greene was not the only one at Mabie Tavern who was impressed, if not seduced, by André's engaging fortitude and charm. Washington's young aide, the worldly and sophisticated Alexander Hamilton, who had waxed rhapsodically at Robinson House over the tender plight of Arnold's beautiful wife, was no less taken by André's sad plight at Mabie Tavern. In each case, he saw attractive and sympathetic young people caught up in the tragic circumstances of war. Of André, who he had been assigned by Washington to watch over while he was a prisoner at Tappan, Hamilton wrote:

> There was something singularly interesting in the character and fortunes of André. To an excellent understanding, well improved by education and travel, he united the peculiar elegance of mind and manners, and the advantage of a pleasing person.... His knowledge appeared without ostentation, and embellished by a diffidence that rarely accompanies so many talents and accomplishments, which left you to suppose more than appeared. His elocution was handsome; his address easy, polite and insinuating. By his merit, he had acquired the unlimited confidence of his general.[75]

Hamilton was not the only American to be seduced by the winning Englishman during his captivity. Major Benjamin Tallmadge, another of Washington's bright young officers, who served his commander as head of the intelligence network in the neutral zone and was, as we have seen, the first American officer to recognize clearly that André was a spy, was also sympathetic to André. He had been sent by Washington to interrogate the prisoner at Lower Salem. When he had finished, he said to Colonel Samuel Webb, another intelligence officer who had known André previously:

> By heavens, Colonel Webb, I never saw a man whose fate I foresaw whom I so sincerely pitied. He is a young fellow of the greatest accomplishments, and was the prime minister of Sir Harry [General Henry Clinton] on all occasions. He has unbosomed his heart to me and, indeed, let me know every motive of his actions....He has endeared himself to me exceedingly. Unfortunate man! He will undoubtedly suffer death...and though he knows his fate, seems to be as cheerful as if he was going to an assembly. I am sure he will go to the gallows less fearful of his fate and with less

---

[75] Flexner, op. cit, 383.

concern than I shall behold the tragedy. Had he been tried by a court of ladies, he is so genteel, handsome, polite a young gentleman I am confident they would have acquitted him.[76]

On September 28, just five days after André's capture at Tarrytown, high-ranking officers appointed by Washington began to convene at Mabie Tavern for the trial, officially termed an "inquiry." This was an impressive gathering, clear testimony that Washington was aware of the significance of the event. To hang one of the highest-ranking officers on General Clinton's staff for the crime of spying could have serious repercussions at home and abroad. There must be no question about the quality of the court that examined him, although Washington himself had, by all accounts, prejudged the case and found André guilty. The commander-in-chief assembled the best he had. He appointed General Greene, arguably the most able of his officers, to preside. For international legitimacy, he added two widely respected figures, the French boy-wonder, the Marquis de Lafayette and the Prussian, Baron von Stueben. Three other major-generals on the court were William Alexander (the self-styled Lord Sterling), Arthur Sinclair, a Scotsman who had fought in the French and Indian War and Robert Howe who, like many of his fellow generals, had once been a British officer.[77]

As if six officers of the highest rank were insufficient to comprise the court membership, Washington added eight more of the next highest rank, brigadier-general. These included Henry Knox, John Stark, John Glover, Sam Parsons, John Patterson, Jedidiah Huntington, James Clinton and Edward Hand—a group of officers with a wide range of skills and combat experience. The board was an honor roll of American military talent.

The trial began the next day at the nearby Old Dutch Church. André had already been briefed on what would transpire by the man who would prosecute the case, Colonel John Lawrence, the army's judge advocate. This was to be an inquiry into all aspects of what André and Arnold had conspired to accomplish. The

---

[76] Ibid., 385.
[77] For an account of the trial see Van Doren, op. cit., 355 ff.

purpose of the proceeding was to ascertain whether André was a spy and if so what punishment he should receive. The prisoner would be allowed to make a statement to this board of inquiry, in writing if he liked. If he wished to call any witnesses on his behalf, they would be summoned. Although members of the board would question him vigorously, he would not be required to name those who had aided him in his actions. When the proceedings were completed, probably in a day or two, the board would make a recommendation to Washington who might accept or reject the findings as he saw fit.

There is little doubt that most members of the board knew that Washington had already decided that, regardless of their findings, André would hang. Certainly General Greene was well aware that his commander, filled to overflowing with anger at the conspiracy, had already made up his mind. The only thing that might save André was Washington's desire to get his hands on the hated Arnold. If that meant giving up André in exchange for return of the traitor by Clinton, Washington might agree. He wanted to hang them both but if he could only get one he would take the now despised Arnold.

Meantime, however, the trial proceeded on schedule. Tallmadge, with a squad of six soldiers, escorted the prisoner from the tavern to the church and, on entering, motioned him to a table and chair set in front of an intimidating row of fourteen uniformed generals. Lawrence began the proceedings by reading a message from Washington setting forth his charge to the court and his summary of the bare facts of the case: the prisoner had come behind American lines at night under an assumed name, had held discussions with General Arnold during which he received confidential military information, had then donned a disguise and been taken prisoner while trying to escape back into British-held territory with the incriminating papers still in his possession. Washington charged the board to ascertain the relevant facts, determine what crime the prisoner had committed and recommend a suitable punishment.

Next, Lawrence read into the record a copy of André's letter to Washington, written on the twenty-fifth from South Salem, a letter in which the prisoner claimed to be a British officer and not a spy and hence available for humane treatment rather than hanging. In that letter, André had spelled out the chronology of events leading up to and following his meeting with Arnold. He was a British officer under orders from his commander to go behind enemy lines and meet with an enemy general to discuss ways in which that general might aid the British war effort. He was as surely acting under recognized rules of war as if he had been leading a troop of men into combat within enemy territory. He arrived dressed as a British officer and met Arnold along the shore with the intention of returning at once to his ship.

André continued his version of relevant facts. He had taken off his uniform, assumed a disguise and traveled through American-held territory against his will. He had been ordered to do so by General Arnold's agent (Joshua Hett Smith, whose name André did not divulge to the board.) This same unnamed agent was the man who had fetched him from the *Vulture*, brought him to Arnold, kept him overnight in his house and then been his guide through American territory. André further declared that he had never acted on his own initiative to disguise his identity as a British officer but was required by circumstances to obey the agent (Smith) and so was in no way so unworthy as to be called a spy.

Unfortunately for André, he had no knowledge of two other accounts of the events in question that had been sent in recent days to Washington from men who were almost as intimately involved in the entire affair as André himself: Benedict Arnold and Beverly Robinson. In their eagerness to extricate André, they had both, after consultation with General Clinton, stressed the fact that André had come under a flag of truce and so was not a spy but a military officer behaving openly as a representative of the British commander to an American general. As such, André should never have been held as a prisoner, much less tried as a spy.

When asked by the court, which had received the two letters using the flag-of-truce defense but had not shared them with André, whether he had come under a flag of truce, André told the truth and said that he had not. Had he done so, he said, he would have returned safely under that flag. No, his defense was that he had behaved as a British officer at all times and as such might be detained but should be treated as a prisoner of war and not as a spy. Even if André had been aware of the false story told by his friends, he probably would not have used it as a defense. He was shrewd enough to realize that a flag of truce only protected those carrying messages to the enemy and was never meant to shield the sort of activities in which he had been engaged.

The well-meaning flag-of-truce letters from Arnold and Robinson had accomplished nothing but to cast further suspicion on André who was now seen as caught up in a web of lying and deceit. As for his defense that his behavior was akin to that of any British officer leading men into enemy territory, this the board regarded as nonsense. Clearly here was a man who was the head of spying operations for the British; had been caught behind American lines while in disguise and using an assumed name; was hiding in his boots sensitive military information that he had acquired from an American general; and was on his way back to British headquarters in New York to deliver that information to the enemy. Furthermore, the defendant admitted all of these facts. There was only one name for such a man: Spy!

After a short deliberation, the board read its verdict to the defendant:

> Major André, Adjutant General of the British Army, ought to be considered a spy from the enemy, and that, agreeable to the law and usage of nations…he ought to suffer death.[78]

On the day after the trial, Washington approved the verdict. He ordered that André be hanged within twenty-four hours.

In the hours following the sentence, André spoke only well of his American captors and judges, saying that he had been treated in a polite and gentlemanly manner throughout the proceedings. His only regret was that he had brought distress upon his commander, Sir Henry Clinton. His request for permission to write to Clinton was granted. In that letter, he absolved his commander of responsibility for the actions that had led to his capture and trial, expressed his gratitude for Clinton's many kindnesses and asked him to help his mother and sisters when he was gone.[79]

Shortly after the verdict was read to him, André wrote an appeal to Washington—a man he had never met—requesting the

---

[78] Flexner, op. cit., 384.
[79] Van Doren, op. cit., 475.

dignity of being shot as an enemy officer and not hanged as a
common spy:

> Buoyed above the terror of death by the consciousness of a
> life devoted to honorable pursuits, and stained with no
> action that can give me remorse, I trust that the request I
> make to Your Excellency at this serious period, and which
> is to soften my last moments, will not be rejected.

> Sympathy toward a soldier will surely induce Your
> Excellency and a military tribunal to adapt the mode of my
> death to the feelings of a man of honor.

> Let me hope, sir, that if aught in my character impressed
> you with esteem toward me, if aught in my misfortunes
> marks me as the victim of policy and not of resentment, I
> shall experience the operation of these feelings in your
> breast by being informed that I am not to die on the gibbet.[80]

Despite Alexander Hamilton's earnest support of André's
request, Washington went ahead with plans for the hanging. To
have done otherwise would be to credit André's argument that he
was not a spy and to fuel the growing sentiment on his behalf,
even in the ranks of his own officer corps. Washington did,
however, delay the execution for several days. He was awaiting
word from Clinton on his informal offer to exchange André for
Arnold.

A Traitor for a Spy

A prisoner exchange was not Washington's only option for
achieving what was now his primary objective—other than
winning the war—which was to see that the traitor was executed.
Some of his advisors suggested sending an undercover squad to
find Arnold and assassinate him. Washington prohibited this
approach. Another idea was to attempt a kidnapping. This
stratagem was the one Washington favored. But meantime he sent
a trusted young aide, Colonel Aaron Ogden, with a verbal message
for Clinton. If the British commander would return Arnold, the

---

[80] Flexner, op. cit., 386-7.

American commander would release André immediately. Ogden returned shortly with Clinton's negative response. Clinton did, however, wish to send General Robertson and two other officers to meet privately with Washington or his designees to discuss the affair.

On October 1, Washington dispatched General Greene, along with Alexander Hamilton and two other officers, to meet Robertson who disembarked from a British ship at Sneden's Landing near Tappan across the river from Dobb's Ferry. The meeting between Greene and Robertson took place along the shore. For over an hour the two enemies parlayed. The British general insisted that André was, by all civilized rules of warfare, not a spy and Greene insisted that he was. Robertson offered to release a number of high Americans then in captivity in return for André's freedom. Greene replied that it was Arnold for André or nothing. The last hope for an exchange died as General Robertson returned to his ship and sailed back to New York.

Although the exchange failed, the kidnapping plot almost worked. In early October, Washington began plotting with General "Light-Horse" Harry Lee to have one of Lee's trusted men, Sergeant Major John Champe, pretend defection to the British and join Arnold's unit of fellow deserters then forming in New York. On October 20, Champe caught up with Arnold on a city street and told him that he was so inspired by the actions of the former West Point commander that he too had decided to switch sides and join his hero in fighting for the British. Gaining Arnold's trust and access to his house, Champe was able to slip into the garden unobserved and loosen some of the pickets on the fence surrounding it so that he could easily remove them when, at some opportune moment, he would overpower Arnold and drag him out of the garden. The plan was to grab the general as he took his regular evening walk in his garden, and carry him bound and gagged to the waterfront, claiming that he was a drunken sailor being taken to the guard house. Then Champe would get him into a waiting boat and across the river to the American lines in New Jersey.

The opportune moment never came. The day before the trap was to be sprung, Champe, along with other members of Arnold's new legion, was put aboard a ship sailing to Virginia where

André being led to execution

Courtesy of the Emmet Collection, Miriam and Ira D. Wallach Division of Arts, Prints and Photographs, The New York Public Library, Astor, Lenox and Tilden Foundations.

André hanged

Arnold would soon join them to take up fighting against rebel forces in the South. Several other plots to capture Arnold also failed but none came as close as Champe's attempt. Washington issued standing orders to all his commanders that if Arnold were ever caught he was to be summarily executed. But the traitor was never trapped except, perhaps, in the prison of his own conscience.

The Stuff of Legends

On October 2, eight days after his capture and three days after his trial, John André was hanged at Tappan. He was marched in a procession of soldiers from his room at Mabie Tavern to the site of the execution. The funeral march was played and the prisoner, resplendent in his British officer's uniform and marching proudly down the road, seemed in better spirits than those who were about to execute him. A large crowd of spectators filled the fields along his route. Witnesses later testified to his calm and grace in the face of his imminent and grizzly end. He was determined not to act the part of a spy in death and would deport himself, as he always had, as an officer and a gentleman.

Benjamin Tallmadge, who had by this time become André's friend, reported later that he had "walked with him to the place of execution and parted with him under the gallows, entirely overwhelmed with grief that so gallant an officer and so accomplished a gentleman should come to such an ignominious end."[81]

As he approached the gallows, André noticed that the officers who had condemned him were lined up along the road. He bowed courteously to them and they returned the gesture. Then he looked up and saw the gallows. For the first time he realized that he would not be shot as a gentleman but hanged as a spy. Horrified, he lost his composure for a moment. "Must I die in this way?" he cried. When told that he must, he exclaimed in a loud voice, "I am reconciled to my fate but not to the mode." Asked if he had any final words, André replied, "I have nothing more to say,

---

[81] Van Doren, op. cit., 355

gentlemen, but this: you all bear me witness that I meet my fate as a brave man."[82]

With that, the Englishman climbed, unaided, onto the back of the horse-drawn wagon that was positioned under the gallows. The executioner then appeared; he was an altogether crude, filthy, uncouth character, about as stark a contrast in appearance and bearing to the prisoner as could be imagined. André pulled the noose over his own neck and pulled it tight. He then covered his eyes with a handkerchief and waited calmly as the hangman climbed one of the supporting posts and tied the other end of the rope to the crossbar.

The crowd fairly moaned as they watched the executioner drop to the ground, apply his whip to the horses and the wagon pull away leaving John André dangling in the cool air of the autumn afternoon.

Alexander Hamilton wrote of André, shortly after witnessing the execution, that "among the extraordinary circumstances that attended him, in the midst of his enemies, he died universally esteemed and universally regretted."[83]

While some Americans, like Hamilton and Tallmadge were celebrating André's courage, the British commander, Sir Henry Clinton was using these words to describe his American counterpart:

> The horrid deed is done. W [Washington] has committed premeditated murder [and] he must answer for the dreadful consequences...he is become a murderer and a Jesuit, God grant me patience.[84]

Thus was born the enduring legend of John André, a near epic tale of British courage and honor in the face of crude, traitorous and insensitive American behavior. An English officer and gentleman dies with dignity while one American general betrays his people and skulks away a traitor and another is so intemperately enraged that he ignores civilized rules of warfare in the face of appeals to his honor and sense of justice. And all of this

---

[82] Flexner, op. cit., 392-3.

[83] Van Doren, op. cit., 355.

[84] Ibid., 480, quoting Clinton's letter of October 18, 1780, to his sisters.

set in motion because a crude, semiliterate American vagabond named John Paulding, along with two men of similarly low character, could not extract enough booty from his captive to satisfy his greed.

A contrary legend was born simultaneously. At the time, not everyone shared the assessment of André as tragic hero, Washington as murderer and Paulding and his companions as greedy opportunists. By no means. In fact, George Washington wrote to Congress immediately after André's execution that, although he did not yet know the names of those who had captured Major André, he did know that they had "acted in such a manner upon the occasion as does them the highest honor, and proves them to be men of great virtue." A week later, Washington wrote to Congress again with a full report of the trial and with these words of commendation for André's captors:

> I now have the pleasure to communicate the names of the three persons who captured Major André, and who refused to release him, notwithstanding the most earnest importunities and assurance of a liberal reward on his part. Their names are John Paulding, David Williams, and Isaac Van Wart.
>
> Their conduct merits our warmest esteem, and I beg leave to add that I think the public would do well to allow them a handsome gratuity. They have prevented in all probability our suffering the severest strokes that could have mediated against us.[85]

On November 3, less than six weeks after André's capture and barely a month after his execution, Congress passed the following resolution:

> *Whereas,* Congress have received information that John Paulding, David Williams, and Isaac Van Wart, three young volunteer militia-men of the State of New York, did on the 23rd day of September last, intercept Major John André, Adjutant-General of the British Army, on his return from the American lines in the character of a Spy; and,

---

[85] Walsh, op. cit., 153.

notwithstanding the large bribes offered them for his release, nobly disdaining to sacrifice their country for the sake of Gold, secured and conveyed him to the Commanding officer of the district, whereby the dangerous and traitorous conspiracy of Benedict Arnold was brought to light, the insidious designs of the enemy baffled, and the United States rescued from impending danger,

Resolved, That Congress have a high sense of the virtuous and Patriotic conduct of the said John Paulding, David Williams and Izaac Van Wart: *In Testimony whereof:*

Ordered, That each of them receive annually out of the Public Treasury Two Hundred Dollars in specie, an equivalent in current money of these United States, during life, and that the Board of War procure for each of them a silver Medal, on the one side of which shall be a Shield with this inscription: *"Fidelity,"* and on the other the motto, *"Vincit Armor Patriae"*—and forward them to the Commander in Chief, who is requested to present the same, with a copy of this Resolution, and the thanks of Congress for their Fidelity, and the eminent service they have rendered their country.[86]

Thus began the elevation to the stature of national hero of three ordinary farmers from Westchester County, New York, and especially of John Paulding. It was "Patriot John," as he soon came to be known, whose deeds would earn the highest accolades. He was the man who had saved America from certain defeat in her struggle for independence on that fateful day in late September of 1780.

---

[86] Ibid., 153-4.

CHAPTER 10

Escape

The Perils of Being a Patriot

Four of the major figures in this drama of treachery—Benedict and Peggy Arnold, Joshua Hett Smith and Beverly Robinson—all had more success than John André in their efforts to escape the consequences of their complicity in the events of September 23, 1780, and the days immediately preceding and following.

As for John Paulding, he never imagined that he would have to escape anything but the continuous accolades of his country, his state and his immediate neighbors. His actions were so universally acclaimed that he was a hero within days of André's capture. He had married his fifteen-year-old sweetheart, Sarah Tidd (Teed), in April, 1781, just four months after capturing André. The couple settled into the farmstead between Peekskill and Crompond (Yorktown Heights) given John by New York in gratitude for his actions in saving the Republic.

Paulding did not spend all of his time working his new land. His bride, the daughter of a Tory-leaning neighbor, was a lively girl, strong enough to carry on alone with the field work while her famous husband was away. The plot to take the Hudson Valley by treachery had failed, but the British had not gone home. War continued intermittently in the neutral ground and John Paulding was involved in many skirmishes. During 1782 a virtual civil war between Cowboys and Skinners broke out in earnest despite the fact that the war was effectively over when General Cornwallis surrendered at Yorktown, Virginia, in October of the previous year.

In January 1783, just weeks after the British and Americans had agreed to terms of a peace settlement negotiated by John Adams, John Jay and Benjamin Franklin, Paulding was part of what was to be the last raiding party out of Peekskill under the command of John Odell, one of the most famous of rebel leaders in the neutral ground. They had attacked a band of Cowboys, seized their loot and been about to sell it to local farmers near Sing Sing (Ossining) when a loyalist troop under the command of the most notorious of all Cowboy leaders, James DeLancey, discovered and quickly overwhelmed them with a superior force.

Most of Paulding's companions were captured at once, but he fled across the ice of a nearby pond, fearful that if recognized as the heralded American hero—the captor of Major André—he would be physically abused, perhaps tortured or even killed on the spot. One of De Lancey's men spotted him as he was running away and ordered him to stop and identify himself. Paulding replied that he would surrender if his life were spared.

"What is your name?" his pursuer shouted across the distance between them.

"I ran as fast as I could," Paulding shouted back, pretending to have heard a different question.

"I said, What is your name?"

Again, Paulding gave a nonsensical response.

This time, one of the men, running up alongside Paulding, recognized him.

"This is the man who did André," he shouted as he drew his sword and slashed Paulding across the head meaning to kill him.

Paulding fell to the ice where he stood, blood gushing from a severe wound in his head. In a few minutes he was conscious and rose slowly to find himself surrounded by angry men apparently intent on killing him. They cut the band on his pants to keep him from running away and continued to beat him until, suddenly, Paulding's wife's brother, Isaac, who like his father was a British sympathizer who sometimes raided with Cowboy bands, burst into the group.

"Don't kill this man. He is my sister's husband," Isaac pleaded with his fellows.

The Cowboys finally relented. Some of them led the tightly bound and badly wounded patriot down the Post Road to New

York for his third imprisonment. The war might be all but over, but Sir Guy Carleton, Clinton's replacement as British Commander in New York since March 1782, had no intention of turning free such a prized captive, one of the heroes of the rebel cause. He knew that the intrepid Paulding had escaped twice before and so ordered him held in the closest possible confinement at an undisclosed location.[87]

This time, Paulding's "escape" was not dramatic. His wounds healed, he was simply free to go home when the war ended officially in September 1783, with the signing of the Treaty of Paris and the subsequent departure of the British from New York.

Joshua Smith: An Innocent…?

John André was not the only quixotic gentleman to be caught up in the web of conspiracy surrounding Benedict Arnold. The Englishman had an American counterpart who shared his incredible encounter with destiny in the neutral zone along the road to Tarrytown. This was Joshua Hett Smith, another well-educated and traveled gentleman of French ancestry, one whose family had come from France to America rather than to England earlier in the century. As we have seen, the lives of the two young men intersected fatefully in late September when the handsome American lawyer fetched the handsome British adventurer-poet from the *Vulture*, opened his house for the meeting with Arnold, convinced André to don a disguise and then personally guided him through American lines and on his way to the safety of British-held territory.

Washington learned of Smith's complicity in the treason at the same time that he was informed of Arnold's betrayal and André's capture. He immediately ordered the arrest and trial of Smith. The lawyer was at the Haverstraw home of his wealthy brother-in-law, Colonel Ann Hawkes Hay, when he was taken early on Tuesday morning, September 26, scarcely three days since he had left "Mr. Anderson" on the road to Tarrytown. Brought under guard to Arnold's headquarters at Robinson House, he was confronted by the formidable trio of Washington, Knox and Lafayette. They told

---

[87] Meade, op. cit., 276-7.

him that he would probably be hanged for treason. Not knowing that André had been captured and that Arnold was a fugitive, Smith protested that he had done nothing wrong and that Arnold would vouch for him. Washington replied that Arnold was a traitor and that Smith's only hope for avoiding the gibbet was to confess everything that he and others had done to abet the treason.

In the face of questioning, Smith maintained his innocence of anything more than being a link in a chain of intelligence stretching between the English commander in New York and the American commander at West Point. His role was only to facilitate communication between Clinton's representative, a "Mr. John Anderson," and General Arnold. He knew nothing of the nature of the intelligence passing between the two men and assumed that, since Arnold had requested that he perform this service, everything he had done was in the cause of helping the American war effort. Whether true or not, this was a highly plausible story.

But Washington and his two colleagues did not believe Smith. By this time the countryside was abuzz with talk of Arnold's treason. Everyone, including the American high command, was out for blood. Anyone connected with the plot was suspect and assumed to be guilty. Smith was especially despised because, unlike André, he was an American and also because his family was known for being loyalist sympathizers, especially his famous and wealthy older brother, William Smith, Jr., who, in addition to serving as the chief justice of New York, was a renowned historian and author.[88]

Joshua Smith was of a prominent New York clan. His father had been a prosperous merchant as well as a judge in the New York Supreme Court, a pillar of the Presbyterian Church in New York and a trustee of Princeton University. His mother's family, the Hetts, were no less the Calvinist achievers, arriving in the city as Huguenots from Rochelle, France, earlier in the century. As a

---

[88] The best account of Smith's life and alleged treason is Richard Koke, *Accomplice to Treason: Joshua Hett Smith and the Arnold Conspiracy*, New York, 1973.

boy, Joshua had enjoyed visiting his grandfather, René Hett, a successful merchant who resided on Pearl Street in New York.[89]

Joshua was the underachiever of the family. After his father died in 1769, the twenty-year-old left home. He never finished college but did eventually read for the law and managed to acquire a license to practice in New York. In 1778, he left the city and traveled to Charleston, South Carolina, to marry the 16-year-old step-daughter of his sister Catherine. By early 1780, he had returned to the family estates at Haverstraw and settled into the life a wealthy young Hudson Valley gentleman, continuing to avoid involvement in the war as much as possible while enjoying the manly sports of hunting and fishing and spending as little time as possible at his law practice.

Joshua could not, of course, altogether avoid the war for independence that swirled around him. His hospitality at his riverside mansion at Haverstraw and his discretion were relied upon, but he was not fully trusted by either side in the war. New York's governor, George Clinton, described him as a "loose" character, and some American officers, including Arnold's aide, Richard Varick, as we have seen, thought him to be a totally untrustworthy confidant. Although Smith's personal involvement in the war effort had been limited, he was not an avowed loyalist like most of his family and many of his friends. He served as a member of the New York Committee of Safety during the war but attended very few of its meetings. When the British moved up the Hudson into Haverstraw Bay in the fall of 1777, Joshua was in a position to observe at close hand the movements of British ships, troops and supplies in the region and report the same to the commander at West Point, General Robert Howe. When Arnold succeeded Howe in August of 1780, Smith simply continued this service for the new commander.

Such was the man who had offered Benedict Arnold his good offices and his commodious house, first as temporary refuge and lodging for his wife, Peggy, as she traveled with her infant son from Philadelphia to join her husband at West Point, and later for what is to be, arguably, the most treacherous act in American

---

[89] He was a neighbor on Pearl Street of this writer's ancestor, Ambroise Sicard, another French Huguenot from Rochelle.

history. Whether Smith was a naive victim of circumstances who, as he claimed, was innocent of all wrongdoing, or a co-conspirator with Arnold may never be known. A recent biographer believes Smith's claim, made at his trial and confirmed by Arnold, that he had been duped by Arnold into believing that he was only helping to woo Beverly Robinson and other loyalists away from the British to the American side by opening intelligence channels with them.[90]

...Or Opportunist?

In any event, it is hard to believe that Smith was not at least partially aware of what he was about in serving as André's host and guide. He had met André at close quarters earlier in the war and credibility is strained to think that he did not recognize the man he had met only four years before. As for Smith's self-serving writings later in life, while he was living in exile in England, to the effect that George Washington was an evil man and André a great romantic hero, these clearly were intended to ingratiate himself with the English and served only to confirm the beliefs of most of his American countrymen that he was indeed a traitor who should have been hanged with André.

Following his interrogation by Washington, Lafayette and Knox, Smith was held overnight at the Robinson house and then spent several days in prison cells at West Point and Stony Point while en route, along with André, to trial at Tappan. He was held in the Dutch Church there while André was secured in the nearby Mabie Tavern. The court for his trial consisted of thirteen judges—most of the rank of only captain—and Judge Advocate General John Lawrence who served as prosecutor. Smith was given no defense attorney and had to represent himself. The charge was treason.

Witnesses testifying against him included Alexander Hamilton, General Knox and General Lafayette. His servants, the uncooperative Cohoon brothers, Joseph and Samuel, who had balked at rowing André back out to the *Vulture*, were also called to testify as were two of André's captors, John Paulding, and

---

[90] Ibid., 58-64.

David Williams. The Cohoons' testimony, although not directly relevant to the charges against Smith, did serve to provide first-hand accounts of André's capture. Smith heard for the first time eyewitness accounts of what had happened to André after he had left him at Pine's Bridge.

Paulding's and Williams' testimony allowed the prosecutor to offer in evidence the fact that André was indeed a spy and also that one piece of material they had found on his person was a memo written by Arnold that included Smith's name as the one in charge of some sort of mission. For whatever reason, Smith did not choose to cross-examine the two captors of André. Perhaps he did not want to open up the question of the meaning of that ambiguous memo.[91]

After ten days of trial, Smith became ill. He was transported to Totowa, New Jersey, where the trial resumed and continued for another six days during which the defendant brought in character witnesses who testified that he had never tried to conceal any of his activities related to setting up communication lines between Arnold and Clinton. In a brilliant summation, Smith contended that he had been denied his right to trial by jury and should be acquitted on that ground alone. The court found him guilty of conspiracy but decided that there was insufficient evidence that he ever knew of Arnold's intentions to do anything more than communicate with Clinton. He was acquitted.

Washington, however, had no intention of releasing Smith. Like the general public, the commander-in-chief did not believe that Smith was so naive as to be ignorant of what Arnold was up to. In the event, Washington did not even inform the prisoner of the verdict. He simply imprisoned him in the jail at West Point where he was badly treated, fed poor food and deprived of the most basic rights of prisoners. After several months, he was transferred to the prison at Goshen, New York, and his case was turned over to the New York Provincial Government for possible retrial. Here he was held for six months until May of 1781.

By the time of his second trial Smith had endured more than a year of harsh imprisonment. He was physically ill and seriously depressed. At this trial, a grand jury found insufficient evidence

---

[91] Ibid., 154.

even to indict him. Nevertheless, by this time, near war's end, a virtual frenzy of revenge-seeking had developed in the public as more and more British sympathizers were being rounded up for trials in which various sorts of retribution were sought.

On the night of May 20, 1781, Smith's ever-faithful wife, Ella, who had been allowed to share his prison quarters, stuffed her husband's side of their bed with whatever was at hand to deceive any guards who might look into their room before dawn. Joshua Smith slipped out into the darkness and began his long and dramatic escape to freedom. For two harrowing weeks he hid in fields, forests, farmhouses and was nearly captured several times with his pursuers always close behind. Several times, sympathetic guides led him through unfamiliar territory. Once he disguised himself as a woman. Finally, on June 4, he was safely within British lines at the New York City home of his older brother, the loyalist Judge William Smith. Here his wife and children soon joined him, traveling from their home at Haverstraw. The Smiths lived in a state of near-poverty amidst the frenetic exit of the British from the city at the close of the war.

In late 1783, the Smith brothers sailed for England. Joshua took his children with him but left his wife behind. Ella was seriously ill at the time and probably could not have withstood the rigors of an Atlantic crossing. This remarkable young woman of genteel southern birth died shortly after bidding her husband and children farewell at the New York dockside. She was just thirty years old.

Once safely in England, Joshua Smith as much as admitted his complicity in treason by seeking reimbursement from the Crown for his losses in the service of Britain. The British doubted his loyalty as much as the Americans had. He was discredited all-around and soon fell into such a state of poverty that he barely escaped debtor's prison. Brother William fared much better since his loyalty to England had been less equivocal. In 1785 he was appointed Chief Justice of Canada and returned to the North American continent to live out his years. Joshua lived in England for most of the next thirty years except possibly for a brief stint in Canada in the 1890's. He remarried and practiced law in the remote village of Shepton Mallet in Somerset, north of Exeter.

Here in southwest England Smith published, in 1808, his long and rambling panegyric to John André entitled, *An Authentic Narrative of the Causes which Led to the Death of Major André*. His hope to win favor with his new countrymen by extolling their hero, André, while at the same time affirming his own loyalist behavior, failed completely. The work was seen for what it was: a self-serving and largely unbelievable attack by an American on two great leaders of his own country, George Washington and Alexander Hamilton. Shortly after the failure of his book, Smith returned secretly to New York City. Here he lived quietly for about seven years until his death at the ripe age of 69 on October 10, 1818. He was buried in the Dutch Church on Nassau Street.

Meanwhile, the man who was unambiguously Arnold's co-conspirator, the loyalist Colonel Beverly Robinson, was arrested by the Americans after the war but soon released without ever being tried for treason. The British subsequently awarded him a generous £17,000 grant ($57,000; about $350,000 in current money) as compensation for his property losses—almost three times the payment Arnold would receive—and gave him a government post in New Brunswick, Canada. After a few years he moved to England and lived out his life peacefully until he died at his home in Bath, not far from Sheppton Mallet where Joshua Smith would later live for a time and practice law.

Arnold, the Free Man

Benedict Arnold had had no more luck than Joshua Smith in his attempts to justify his actions by taking up the pen. Back in New York City from his flight down the Hudson in September of 1780 he set about immediately to write a defense of himself in a tract published in the *Royal Gazette* entitled, "To the Inhabitants of America." Even more self-serving and filled with half-truths than Smith's effort at justification, Arnold's piece similarly failed to convince his new masters of his loyalty to them. Sir Henry Clinton turned down the traitor's request for the full £10,000 originally requested through André as compensation for losses he claimed he had suffered during the war on behalf of the British. Clinton did, however, honor his promise to give Arnold the £6,000 he had authorized as payment, plus a bit more. Given Arnold's failure to deliver, this was a generous payment.

Arnold was made a brigadier general in the British army, a rank lower than he thought he deserved, with an annual pay of £450 and a guarantee of half that amount when he retired, plus an additional £200 a year until the end of the war. Later, two of his sons, Henry and David, received life pensions from the Crown in the amount of £75 a year. As usual, Arnold regarded all of this as inadequate recompense for his services and continued his lifelong resentment at being, as he saw it, an unappreciated man. Nevertheless, he served his new masters well, divulging vital military intelligence including the names and locations of American spies and sympathizers among the loyalists. He also actively recruited soldiers for the British army, promising them clemency and better pay.

Quickly given command, Arnold sailed for Virginia in December 1780 and enjoyed some success in battles there. Governor Jefferson offered a reward for his capture, and Washington sent Lafayette into Virginia with specific instructions to kill Arnold on sight, reversing his earlier disapproval of such action. For a time Arnold was commander at Portsmouth but was discontented with this position and was generally disliked by his men. In August 1781, he was sent to lead a raid in his native state of Connecticut at New London. Once again, he was a success on the battlefield inflicting considerable damage on his former countrymen.

In December 1781, along with General Cornwallis and other high officers, Arnold abandoned the failed British war effort in America and sailed with Peggy and their two children, Edward and James, for England aboard the *Robuste*. Once in England, he sought a commission in the army, citing his service to the Crown and his career as a successful battlefield commander. He would be disappointed. The officer corps was dominated by upper class gentlemen who had purchased their commissions and had no intention of admitting this American plebeian to their ranks. Nor was he able to get a position with any of the British merchant trading companies, despite his experience in that area. He was simply an unwanted person in London, a mistrusted and disliked traitor, a pariah.

Unable to support his growing family in England—Edward and James had been joined by George in 1784 and by sister, Sophia, in 1785—Arnold grew interested in promising opportunities in Canada. A new royal colony was being formed in Nova Scotia, a haven for American Tories who had opposed the revolution but embraced the familiar frontier environment offered in maritime Canada. Perhaps there, in that open climate, ripe with opportunities for men of talent and energy and free of the class snobbery that had thwarted him in England, Arnold might restart his old merchant trading business and, once successful, send for his family.

In December of 1785 Benedict Arnold arrived in St, John, New Brunswick, filled with hope of finally completing his escape from disgrace and poverty. Avoiding the broiling politics of a new colony seeking to define its identity, he concentrated on making money. He had £6 in his pocket—the balance of his payment for treason—and proceeded at once to rent a house, set up a retail store, purchase goods for trade in the West Indies and rent a ship with captain to begin trade while his ship was being built. His plan was to create his own trading empire in which he would own the lumber and other saleable goods as well as the ships that carried them and the warehouses and retail outlets that stored and sold them. He even went so far as to become the supplier of some of the foodstuffs consumed by the crews on his ships.[92]

In a short time, Arnold was achieving considerable success in his ambitious business ventures, trading regularly from New Brunswick and Nova Scotia to the West Indies and often to England as well. He brought his devoted sister, Hannah, and her three charges, his sons by his first wife (Benedict VI, Richard and Henry) to live in St. John. Then, on a trip to England in 1787, he picked up his pregnant wife, Peggy, and her three small children and settled them all into a beautiful house in St. John. They welcomed son George (the first George having died in infancy) shortly after arrival and before long were recognized as the most prosperous family in the colony.

---

[92] For a full account of Arnold's life in Canada, see Barry K. Wilson, *Benedict Arnold: A Traitor In Our Midst,* Montreal, 2001, esp. 165 ff.

By all accounts, Arnold in Canada was a devoted husband, father and brother, enjoying domesticity for the first extended period in his adult life. Peggy felt sufficiently secure in her tranquil new surroundings to visit her family in Philadelphia for about five months in the winter of 1789-90.

But all of this success and contentment was not to last. Arnold, after all, could not escape either his own demons or his reputation as a traitor. Ever the arrogant, aggressive uncompromising egotist, he soon managed to alienate himself from the elite of the colony. In a series of lawsuits he pursued those whom he thought, sometimes rightly, had cheated him in a variety of business dealings. On one occasion he faced countercharges of illegal smuggling. In another lawsuit, he unsuccessfully filed an insurance claim for a suspicious fire set to his warehouse. In some cases he won damages from ship captains and fellow merchants who had, in fact, cheated him, but he never collected because the guilty parties simply fled town.[93]

In 1791 Arnold sought to change his fortunes again and returned to England with his wife and younger children, leaving the older boys behind with sister Hannah. Before long he was in a pistol duel with the Earl of Lauderdale whom he claimed had offended him in a speech in the House of Lords. The earl did not fire his weapon and Arnold missed, perhaps intentionally. The earl apologized and the matter was closed. Once again, however, the temperamental Arnold had displayed his lack of tact and social decorum and further aggravated the general dislike and distrust of him in England.

After a number of failed appeals by himself and Peggy to Prime Minister William Pitt the Younger and to the Crown for employment, Arnold took matters into his own hands and purchased a ship so that he might engage once again in trade with the West Indies. Fortune was not with him. In Guadeloupe in 1794 he was captured by the French and incarcerated in a prison ship in the harbor. Ever the daring man of action, he managed to escape before his scheduled execution by bribing guards, lowering himself into the harbor on a rope, and paddling on a crude raft through the French fleet to a British ship anchored further out in

---

[93] For a detailed account of these lawsuits see Ibid., 191-216.

the harbor. Ironically, he served for a brief time thereafter in the respectable post of quartermaster to Sir Charles Grey, André's old commander in New York.

In the summer of 1795 Arnold returned to England to a much relieved but seriously ill Peggy. She was ailing severely from a malady from which she seems to have suffered all of her life, one described by her husband as a "nervous disorder." While he continued to struggle, without much success, to earn money for his growing family, Peggy was busy ingratiating herself with her new countrymen. Despite her disabilities, she successfully lobbied parliament and the crown for a generous £500 annual stipend for herself and living allowances for her six surviving children. (She had lost two children, George and Margaret in infancy.) Through the good offices of her friend and admirer, Lord Cornwallis, her five sons, Henry, Edward, James, George and William, eventually received commissions in the military, with James and George following their father into army careers, both of them attaining the rank of colonel.[94]

In 1798 Arnold was given a grant by the crown of some 14,000 acres of barren countryside in northern Canada in reward for his services during the Revolution. He didn't live long enough to do much with this questionable prize. The fifty-year-old traitor died in a poor neighborhood in London on June 14, 1801, a bitter and disliked man. He was suffering from a variety of illnesses including asthma, gout, and dropsy and, as Peggy said, "a perturbed mind." Peggy survived him by only three years, laboring until the end to pay off her husband's debts and to secure a good future for their children. She died of an internal tumor at age forty-four and was buried next to her husband in a modest grave at St. Mary's, Battersea on the unfashionable south side of the Thames.[95] Benedict Arnold never escaped after all.

---

[94] Wallace, op. cit., 303.
[95] For account of final years see Ibid., 297-309.

BENEDICT ARNOLD

Benedict Arnold after the Revolution
*Courtesy of Branch Libraries, The New York Public Library,
Astor, Lenox and Tilden Foundations*

— CHAPTER 11 —

Legacies

Some historians have attempted to correct what they see as unfairness in assessments of Benedict Arnold's legacy to America. They have stressed his personal courage and genius as a field commander, especially at the critical battle of Saratoga. He was, before his betrayal, one of Washington's favorite officers, a difficult man to be sure but one who was so brilliant that Washington was willing to shield him from the enemies he had earned with his overweening ambition and arrogant disdain for the necessary give-and-take of human relationships.

A justification offered for Arnold's treason is that he was not alone among those who preferred continued British rule to independence. Many Americans of the day, including some of the most respected and prosperous citizens, remained loyal to England during the American Revolution. But Arnold's situation was quite different. He had been an active revolutionary from the earliest days of the conflict and, later, one of the great heroes of the struggle for independence. He switched sides and betrayed his country's military intelligence not out of any ideological commitment to continued attachment to Britain but from naked and unvarnished greed and ambition, edged with resentment.

Had Arnold been able to temper his ambition and his anger with some political savvy and a bit of patience, his fame as a great warrior might have carried him to the highest levels of American power. Andrew Jackson offers just such an example. Like Arnold, Jackson was a vainglorious, ambitious and courageous war hero whose career was peppered with the scandals of womanizing and physical attacks on, or provoked duels with, rivals over alleged slights and insults. Furthermore, the issue of American independence remained unresolved in the War of 1812 when

Jackson saved the day as the great hero of the Battle of New Orleans, a scarcely less decisive victory for American independence than Arnold's earlier success at Saratoga.

Nor is Andrew Jackson the only military leader in our history who was deeply disappointed and embittered over a perceived lack of appreciation for his talent and heroism. In more recent years, Douglas MacArthur and George Patton come to mind. Such comparisons, though not completely analogous, are instructive. Unlike Arnold, other ambitious and egocentric generals in our history have managed to avoid self-destruction by bridling their egos sufficiently to stay within the pale of loyalty to their country and its system of government if not to the particular leaders of their day. No other great leader of such courage, intelligence and talent as Arnold was so embittered, self-centered and greedy as to let his ambition override his loyalty to his country.

The enduring legacy of Benedict Arnold is his treason. For Americans, he represents the antithesis of patriotism and the epitome of betrayal of country. There is a monument constructed in his honor at the Saratoga battlefield, the scene of his greatest triumph, which describes him as the "most brilliant soldier" of the War for Independence. But his name, which is synonymous with treachery, does not appear anywhere on the monument. So much is he hated and so unthinkable is his treason that his great courage and apparent love of country could not possibly have been displayed by someone named Benedict Arnold.

John André's Legacy

Major John André's memorial monument is in Westminster Abbey in London. His name is on it. Though scarcely remembered today in America, he remains at least a minor hero in English history. In his own time, King George III praised him and awarded his grieving mother a monetary gift. Joshua Hett Smith, as we have seen, tried to elevate him to the level of tragic hero in his self-serving panegyric.

Many English poets extolled André as a martyr. The most notable of these tributes was a work by an important poet of the day, Anna Seward. She called her long, riming tribute, *Monody on the Death of Major André*. In the poem she condemns the

American insurgents, especially the "remorseless Washington" and, with a patriotic fervor characteristic of the day, elevates André to the level of a sacred patriot whose deeds might well inspire his countrymen to fight another day in America to avenge his death.

> Loud howls the storm! The vex'd Atlantic roars!
> Thy Genius, Briton, wanders on its shores!
> Hears cries of horror wafted from afar,
> And groans of Anguish mid the shrieks of war!
> Hears the deep curses of the Great and Brave
> Sigh in the wind and murmur on the Wave...
>
> Remorseless Washington! The day shall come
> Of deep repentance for this barb'rous doom!
> When injured André's memory shall inspire
> A kindling army with resistless fire;
> Each falchion sharpen that the Britons wield
> And lead their fiercest Lion to the field!
> Then, when each hope of thine shall set in night,
> When dubious dread and unavailing flight
> Impel your host, thy guilt-upbraided soul
> Shall wish untouched the sacred life you stole!
> And when thy heart appall'd and vanquished pride
> Shall vainly ask the mercy they deny'd,
> With horror shalt thou meet the fate they gave,
> Nor Pity gild the darkness of thy grave![96]

None of this praise for André by his English compatriots is surprising. He had, after all, not only fought valiantly for his country and nearly succeeded in single-handedly defeating the American cause with his brilliant cunning, but he had also died a martyr, a victim of a sham trial and execution by a people who were so uncouth that they ignored the rules of civilized warfare—or so the English thought.

What may be surprising is the extent to which André was honored by many of his peers among the enemy. Notable among

---

[96] Quoted in Walsh, op. cit., 176-7.

these admirers were two of the young men on Washington's staff who witnessed André's trial and execution. One, as we have seen, was Alexander Hamilton, later secretary of treasury and a presidential aspirant. Hamilton had come under the spell of André's charm and never ceased in his praise for the Englishman's courage and dignity. The other prominent American admirer was Benjamin Tallmadge, the principal overseer of André during his brief imprisonment who later served as a prominent congressman and, as such, acted on his affection and loyalty to André by publicly castigating his captors as rank opportunists and blocking efforts to reward them for their capture of an enemy soldier regarded by most Americans as a nefarious spy.

Such was the spell cast by John André on a number of conservative American leaders who shared their English cousins' disdain for the crude, opportunistic, democratic, classless and often lawless society that they feared might engulf them with the creation of the new state. Men like André's principal captor, the rough John Paulding, seemed to epitomize just this sort of emergent common man as the heroic paradigm for the new America. If they had to choose between the English gentleman, André, and the ordinary farmer, Paulding, as the prototypical new man for their country, they would take the Englishman, spy or no.

The Image of Hero

For most Americans, however, from George Washington to the ordinary citizen, John Paulding was the real hero. His legacy, though all but vanished today, endured for nearly a century as the prototypical common-man hero, the man whose courage, daring and self-sacrifice saved the day, the man who saved America.

Washington personally thanked the captors of André. On the day of the spy's execution he shook their hands. He later informed Congress that by their courage they "have prevented in all probability our suffering one of the severest strokes that could have been meditated against us." If they had not shown such patriotism, "in September 1780, [victory at] Yorktown might have been impossible in October, 1781."[97]

---

[97] Brown, op. cit., 29.

Congress responded, as we have already noted, by praising the men for their "virtuous and patriotic conduct" and by awarding them lifetime annuities.[98] The medals were presented with appropriate ceremony at a special banquet held in their honor. The three men sat next to George Washington and heard many testimonials to their courage and virtue. Washington presented each of them with a sword and a brace of pistols as his personal gifts. He offered them full commissions as captains in the regular army. Williams and Van Wart chose to leave military service altogether. Only Paulding returned to active duty with the Westchester militia and, as we have seen, was badly wounded and captured in a skirmish near Sing Sing and imprisoned by the British for a third time.

By the time of the Treaty of Paris and Paulding's release from prison in September of 1783, his reputation as the first common-man hero of America's struggle for independence was already beginning to emerge. The ink was scarcely dry on the peace treaty when a popular ballad testifying to Paulding's patriotism helped to secure for him the name "Patriot John." Written by John Renfro Davis, the ditty was known variously as *The Ballad of Major André*, *The Execution of Major André* and *Major André's Capture*. First appearing in about 1821, the lyrics began:

> Come, all you brave Americans,
> And unto me give ear,
> I'll sing you now a ditty
> That will your spirits cheer,
> Concerning a young gentleman
> Who came from Tarrytown,
> Where he met a British officer,
> A man of high renown.
>
> Then up spoke this young hero,
> John Paulding was his name;
> 'O tell us where you're going sir,
> And also whence you came.'
> 'I bear the British flag, sir,'

---

[98] Walsh, op. cit., 153-4.

Up answered bold André,
'I have a pass that takes me through,
I have no time to stay.'

The others came around him.
And bade him to dismount;
'Come tell us where you're going,
Give us a strict account;'
Young Paulding said, 'We are resolved
That you shall ne'er pass by':
And so the evidence did prove
The prisoner was a spy.

He begged for his liberty,
He pled for his discharge,
And oftentimes he told them,
If they'd set him at large,
'Of all the gold and silver
I have laid up in store,
But when I reach the city
I will send you ten times more.'

'We scorn this gold and silver
You have laid up in store,'
Van Vert and Paulding both did cry,
'You need not send us more.'

Then round him [André] came, this company,
And bid him to dismount;
"Come, tell us where you're going.
Give us a strict account;
For we are now resolved
That you shall ne'er pass by."
Upon examination
They found he was a spy.

....

A bumper to John Paulding!

Now let your voices sound,
Fill up your flowing glasses,
And drink his health around;
Also to those young gentlemen
Who bore him company;
Success to North America
Ye sons of Liberty![99]

Shortly after the war's end, the State of New York presented Paulding, Williams and Van Wart with farms valued at about £500 each. These properties had been seized from loyalists who had fled during or after the war. Paulding's farm, some 168 prime acres located along Crompound Road just east of Peekskill, had been taken from Dr. Peter Huggeford, a Tory and the first physician in the region. Over the years, Paulding sold off some of his land, one parcel for a new Methodist Church, another for construction of a school house and several to private parties.

In addition to medals, life pensions, land grants and a popular ballad in his honor, Patriot John was celebrated in one of the first popular "Broadway" plays in New York City. Opening at the Park Theatre on July 4, 1803, under the title, *The Glory of Columbia, Her Yeomanry*, the play intended to show, by a detailed if somewhat fictionalized depiction of Arnold's betrayal and André's capture, that it was the American common man who was the true hero of the Revolution. Written by William Dunlap, a noted playwright, poet and painter of day, the production was offered to enthusiastic audiences on the Fourth of July and other special patriotic occasions for nearly fifty years. In 1812 a subtitle was added to make clear that the play was still relevant in a time of continued British threats: *What We Have Done We Can Do*.

John Paulding was featured in the play but not as the major character. A larger role went to André who was treated as a tragic hero. Dunlap had spent time studying in England and no doubt been influenced by the sympathy for André among his English friends. (Earlier, in 1798, he had produced a play set in Tappan, the site of André's trial and execution, called *André: A Tragedy in*

---

[99] Brown, op. cit., 28.

Five Acts. This drama, largely sympathetic to André, ran briefly in New York)

In *Glory of Columbia*, Paulding was given lines that displayed his role as a hero of the Revolution. When he entered, along with Williams and Van Wart, a chorus of male and female peasants filled half the stage and sang a patriotic ballad:

> See they come—the heroes come!
> Hark! The hollow sounding drum!
> Gives distant notes of coming war,
> And bids th'invaders keep afar,
> Or for the battle's brunt prepare.
>
> See the stately horse come prancing,
> There the musketeers advancing,
> While the canoneers prepare
> Thundering war.
> See the standards float
> Hark the trumpets note
> While every breath with conscious might
> Swells ardent for the coming fight.
>
> But now crown the glorious war
> See Washington! The battle's soul!
> His worth binds envy in her cave
> In council sage, in battle brave!
> Great Washington, a world can save![100]

When Paulding is hailed as a hero, he replies modestly that "the thanks of his commander" is all the reward a true soldier ever needs. He continues:

> We must always remember the moment as the most glorious of our lives. The approbation of our country is at all times precious, but when that approbation is made known by such

---

[100] William Dunlap, "The Glory of Columbia Her Yeomanry," in Richard Moody, ed., *Dramas from the American Theater 1762-1909*. Cleveland, 1966, 101.

a man so glorious and so dignified [as Washington] it becomes inestimable.[101]

Another notable literary legacy of John Paulding is James Fennimore Cooper's first successful novel, *The Spy*, which appeared in 1821.

The book is based partially on the events surrounding Arnold, André, Paulding and other players in the real-life drama. Cooper, who is arguably America's first great novelist, set his story in the dangerous neutral ground. He was the first to make widely known the viscous civil war that went on between loyalists and revolutionaries in this critical region. While the historical persons and events are highly fictionalized, we easily recognize that Cooper has drawn heavily upon real events.

John Paulding is one of the characters in the novel who appears as himself. He is portrayed as a heroic figure who resists the temptation to play the usual marauding role of Skinner or Cowboy. Instead he emerges as a selfless patriot. "Don't you think Paulding's party were fools in not letting the Royal Adjutant General [André] escape?" Cooper asks rhetorically. "King George would have made them gentlemen for their lives for he is richer. But, thank God, there is a pervading spirit in people that seems miraculous. Men [like Paulding] who have nothing act as if the wealth of the Indies depends on their fidelity."[102]

A friend and colleague of Cooper's was John Paulding's young cousin, James Kirke Paulding, who was himself one of the most celebrated American writers of the early nineteenth century. A politically active Jacksonian Democrat, James Paulding pioneered an indigenous American literature. Rather than copying English or European themes, he used the experiences of Native Americans and early Dutch settlers to display life in this new frontier environment. He wrote novels, poetry, plays, satires, short stories and literary criticism. The titles of some of his most widely read books display his focus on the new America: *John Bull in America*, 1825; *The Three Wise Men of Gotham*, 1826; *The*

---

[101] Ibid., 100.

[102] James Fennimore Cooper, *The Spy: A Tale of the Neutral Ground*, (1821), New York, 2002, 225.

Dutchman's Fireside, 1831; *Westward Ho!*, 1832; *A Life of Washington*, 1838; *American Comedies*, 1847.

James Paulding memorialized and idolized his older cousin in poems, novels and satirical essays. "Patriot John" epitomized all that James was trying to project as the picture of the new American man. In his poem "The Backwoodsman" (1818), his satire *The New Mirror for Travellers* (1828) and his novel *The Old Continental and the Price of Liberty* (1846) he praised John and his two companions as true common-man heroes and lamented the romanticizing of the English aristocrat André in American literature and art. If he went too far in his praise of cousin John, presenting him as an unbelievably heroic and self-sacrificing patriot, his reasons for doing so went beyond family pride and democratic zeal. He felt the need to defend John from the criticism that was being heaped upon him by one of the most prominent among the idolizers of John André, Congressman Benjamin Tallmadge.

A Tarnished Image

In 1816, Tallmadge denounced Paulding in the halls of Congress as a self-serving fraud. The congressman, as has been noted, had been an officer under Washington during the war. He was stationed at South Salem at the time of André's capture and spent many hours with the Englishman during his captivity and trial, falling almost totally under the spell of the charming prisoner and accepting his version of events. As for Paulding, he was seen by Tallmadge as nothing but a crude and distasteful character whose version of events was unreliable at best.

Paulding's detractor was a native New Yorker, born on Long Island in 1754, graduated from Yale at age nineteen, a volunteer at Lexington at the outbreak of the war and a great admirer of Washington who served bravely in battles on Long Island, and in Philadelphia and Westchester County. The tall, handsome, intelligent young man soon became a favorite of the commander-in-chief. In the summer of 1778, Washington made him the first chief of his new intelligence service and in 1780 gave him his own command of a dragoon of dismounted soldiers and an accompanying cavalry unit.

On September 23, the day of André's capture, Tallmadge had been, by his own account, "marching and countermarching, skirmishing with the enemy, catching cowboys" and had just returned to the regimental headquarters near North Castle (Mount Kisco) when he was informed that a prisoner had been brought in that day by the name of John Anderson."[103] When he learned that Colonel Jameson had sent André on to Arnold at West Point, he insisted, as we have seen, that the prisoner be returned for questioning. As Washington's chief intelligence officer, Tallmadge knew that his commander would depend upon him, above all others, to carry out a careful examination of the prisoner.

During his examinations of André and while observing the prisoner's demeanor through his captivity, trial and execution, Tallmadge formed a lasting impression of the Englishman as a heroic and altogether sympathetic person—a man to whom he "became so deeply attached" that he could "remember no instance whereby my affections were so fully absorbed in any man." This experience with André, which Tallmadge described as "intimate" would forever color and prejudice his views of André's accusers and any who sought to demean André's honor. As far as Tallmadge was concerned, no one could or should ever replace André as the true hero of those critical events of the autumn of 1780 and that included, above all, those ruffians, Paulding, Williams and Van Wart.

After the war, Tallmadge served in Congress for sixteen years, from 1800 to 1816, during the terms of both Jefferson and Madison. He was an Anglophile who opposed the war policies of President Madison and deplored the emergent populism that would soon flower in Jacksonian democracy and was already evident in the pending election of James Monroe, the first of yeoman stock to serve as president.

When Paulding and his companions appealed to Congress in 1816 for an increase in their pensions on the grounds that the original $200 had shrunk to about half its original value in purchasing power, Tallmadge led the fight against their petition. He held himself out as the only reliable eyewitness to events

---

[103] Benjamin Tallmadge, *Memoir of Colonel Benjamin Tallmadge*, New York, 1858, 34-35.

surrounding André's capture. He had been, after all, Washington's chief military intelligence officer and hence was privy to confidential information. In fact, what he offered the Committee on Pensions was André's version of events as the Englishman had related it to him at the time of his interrogation. He simply accepted at face value André's unlikely story that painted Paulding and his compatriots as nothing but rank opportunists who had tried to extort money from him and only when this failed had turned him in to American authorities.

Tallmadge's attack on three men who had been honored as patriots for a generation and were widely regarded as national heroes produced a storm of public controversy in the press. James Kirke Paulding, who would later serve in President Van Buren's cabinet as Secretary of the Navy, entered the fray with his satiric poem "The Backwoodsman." In this and other writings and speeches made during the remainder of his life, he extolled his cousin's virtues and deplored the idolizing of the spy, André, by Tallmadge and others of his social and political ilk. Many members of Congress also defended Paulding and his compatriots and urged a full congressional investigation into Tallmadge's charges. Isaac Van Wart was so hurt and incensed by the accusations that he swore out an affidavit defending himself and swearing that André had offered a bribe which the three had "promptly and immediately refused."[104]

In the end, however, Tallmadge's objection to raising the pensions carried the day. By a vote of 80-53, the full Congress decided that Paulding's service had not really been exemplary much less extraordinary. Rather, Paulding merely

> did his duty faithfully, and for it has been liberally rewarded. However, he did nothing more than his duty; the country expects this much, at least, from everyone and yet it is not expected that she is to support all who have done so… The petitioner was a private soldier when he rendered the services for which he has been thus liberally rewarded; he

---

[104] After leaving Congress in 1816, Tallmadge was an active and founding member of the Society of Cincinnati and served as president of a bank in Litchfield, Connecticut. He died in March 1835.

was neither wounded nor in any way injured nor even exposed to a greater degree of hardship than thousands of soldiers.[105]

Even though the committee recognized that Paulding was "old, had a large family, is very infirm and incapable of hard labor," it decided that it would set a bad precedent to increase pensions of this sort. A year later, Patriot John died, and Tallmadge, no doubt smarting from attacks by Paulding's supporters upon him for being a supporter of André, introduced a motion in Congress to continue Paulding's pension for the benefit of his wife and children. Even this motion was defeated. However, when David Williams died in 1831, Congress did continue his pension for his wife during the remainder of her life.

The long-term result of Tallmadge's attacks on the integrity of Paulding during these pension hearings in 1816 and 1817 was to cast a lasting cloud over Paulding's loyalty and effectively to destroy his place in American history as an unqualified hero of the American War for Independence that Washington had declared him to be in the midst of that conflict. The passage of thirty-five years and the prejudice of one man acting out his biases in the midst of the heated politics of a later day dulled the memory of how absolutely crucial the patriotism of Paulding, Williams and Van Wart had been at a critical moment in American history. To say that they merely did their duty as all good citizens are expected to do is to apply a rigid philosophical standard of stoical morality to the real world of temptation, greed and self-interest. Surely Paulding and his companions were as close to being genuine heroes as real human beings are ever likely to be.

Still, history belongs to those who write it. Despite accolades at the time from Washington and other great men of the day, including Alexander Hamilton, himself an admirer of Major André who described Paulding, Williams and Van Wart as "three simple peasants" who had displayed commendable "virtue and honest sense of duty" in refusing to be bribed, their place in our history had been all but lost.[106] Recent reference works on the American

---

[105] *Annals of Congress*, 1817, XXX, 474-75.

[106] Brown, op. cit., 27.

Revolution give scant or no mention at all of Paulding. When he and his companions are mentioned it is usually in a negative manner. A 1993 work entitled *Who Was Who During the Revolution* describes the three men as part of "a rather scruffy lot" looking for loot who found the papers by accident. The same book describes André as a great man of "nobility and forbearance."[107]

Restoring the Legacy

Despite the disparagement of Patriot John and his companions and the enlargement of André's reputation over the years since Tallmadge's distortions in 1816-17, there remains some evidence in the twenty-first century of Paulding's legacy. There are, for example, the statues and monuments at Tarrytown and at his gravesite in St. Peter's Cemetery at Courtlandville, near Peekskill. The cemetery monument was erected by the City of New York in 1827 and dedicated with great pomp, including speeches by the mayor of New York and Generals Pierre and Philip Van Courtland. In his dedicatory speech, the mayor conjured up the already rapidly developing legend of Patriot John as a folk hero, "the son of a plain country farmer" who

> belongs forever to the yeomanry of the United States, a class of men always honest and of patriotical ways ready to defend the soil in whose products they share liberally, and those rights in which they so amply participate.

Continuing his speech, the mayor recalled that at the time of André's capture:

> the freedom of our country was almost a desperate hope. The money, the credit, the means, may I almost say, the sentiment necessary for continuing the great contest, were either quite exhausted, or fast melting away. The capture of André, while it prevented the most fatal disasters, and led to the most signal results, afforded at the same time a

---

[107] E. Purcell, *Who Was Who in the American Revolution.* New York, 1993, 5, 51; J. Karl, *Who Was Who During the Revolution.* Indianapolis, 1976, 3, 38.

John Paulding after the Revolution
Courtesy of Branch Libraries, The New York Public Library,
Astor, Lenox and Tilden Foundations

John Paulding the Patriot: Statue at Tarrytown, New York
Author's photo

memorable example of the fidelity and patriotism of the yeomanry of these United States.[108]

The man who delivered these sentiments was John Paulding's illustrious cousin, William Paulding, Jr. This Paulding had served as adjutant general of the state, a member of Congress and a major general in the war of 1812 before being elected to two terms as mayor of New York.

The monument on Main Street in the village of Tarrytown is a large marble obelisk located at the sight of the capture of André. Placed there in 1853, the inscription, which appears also on his burial monument in Peekskill, was written by none other that Paulding's ever-admiring cousin, John Kirke Paulding. Patriot John is described as the man who

> Rejecting the temptation of great rewards, conveyed his Prisoner to the American camp. By this act of noble denial, the treason of Arnold was detected, the designs of the enemy baffled, West Point and American Army saved, and the United States, now by the grace of God Free and Independent, rescued from the most imminent peril!

In 1880, on the one-hundredth anniversary of Paulding's fateful act, a life-sized statue of the patriot was affixed atop the Tarrytown monument. Attending that dedication were his son, Rear Admiral Hiram Paulding, Ret., Samuel L. Tilden, the Democratic nominee for president of the United States and a host of other dignitaries and Paulding descendants. A century after the capture and more than sixty years after his death, John Paulding was still a hero to many Americans.

Completing the memorial to Paulding and his compatriots at Tarrytown is a simple New York State historic marker alongside the road entering Tarrytown from the north at about the spot of the historic capture. It reads:

---

[108] Brown, op. cit., 29.

ANDRÉ CAPTURED
HERE IN 1780 THREE HONEST
MILITIAMEN ARRESTED MAJOR
JOHN ANDRÉ ADJ-GEN. BRITISH
ARMY, DISGUISED. PREVENTING
DISASTER TO AMERICAN CAUSE

There have even been movements over the years to erect a permanent monument to Paulding in Washington, D.C. To date all of these efforts have failed to win approval, perhaps because of the cloud that still shrouds his reputation as the captor of the highly romanticized André.

In addition to Broadway plays, ballads and monuments, Paulding's legacy as the great yeoman hero of the Revolution was celebrated for many years in both high art and domestic artifacts. Asker Durand, a founder of the Hudson River school of painting, did the most famous of dozens of paintings of the capture of André. Currier and Ives created prints of Durand's work and more than 10,000 copies were sold. Another painting of the event by Thomas Sully in 1820 is nearly as famous. Images of Paulding's feat also appeared on thousands of plates, pitchers and snuff boxes in shops all over the country.

So enthusiastic was the early recognition of Paulding's importance that streets, schools, fire companies, parks and libraries were named for him, not only in and around Tarrytown and other locales in Westchester County but as far away as Ohio and Georgia. In 1820, Ohio named a new county in the northwest part of the state "Paulding County" in honor of the "Revolutionary War hero, John Paulding." New counties in Ohio were also named for Williams and Van Wart. A similar designation of a new county occurred in Georgia, accompanied by a church, a school and streets named in that state to honor Patriot John. Many other public places throughout the country were named for him throughout the nineteenth century.

Some recent historians have been kind to Paulding's memory. Emma Patterson in her worthy history of Peekskill during the Revolution affirms that "The capture of André...was without doubt the most important single feat in the entire Revolution. For this his [Paulding's] country will always owe him a debt of gratitude." She continues, "Many men who did far less have been more extravagantly rewarded during their lifetimes and have been idealized as heroes after their deaths."[109]

The distinguished historian, Willard Wallace, in his acclaimed biography of Benedict Arnold, writes that although Paulding, Williams and Van Wart were probably "bushwackers" engaged in an "enterprise condemned by both armies...the best that can be said about them is not enough: they may have saved the republic on that Saturday morning."[110]

In the same vein, the popular historian John Evangelist Walsh's recent account of André's capture and execution affirms that

> if it had not been for Paulding and his two companions the story of America would have been vastly different. In halting André that September morning, at a stroke they did more to shape America's future, and in a degree that of the world, than all of the nation's celebrated heroes combined.[111]

We will allow James Kirke Paulding the final words on his cousin's legacy as the prototype of the true heroes of the American War of Independence:

> Those who derive their impressions of the hardships, privations and sufferings of the people of the United States during the war of independence from the general history of the times will form but a vague idea of their magnitude and extension.[112]

> The dark days of the infant Republic had now come. The enemy, everywhere victorious, had overcome, though he could not subdue a large portion of the land.... The paper currency...was fast depreciating...the resources of the country were either exhausted or could not be procured...the little waning army...was struggling without

---

[109] Patterson, op. cit., 139.

[110] Wallace, op. cit., 245.

[111] Walsh, op. cit., 152.

[112] James Paulding, op. cit., 140.

hope, the cradle of the infant "Liberty" seemed on the eve of becoming its grave. But amid all these discouragements and disasters, the great mass of the people, the sturdy yeomanry of the country, remained true to the cause of independence....[113]

And no one more so than Patriot John.

One year after Congress denied his petition for a pension increase, John Paulding died at his farmhouse near Peekskill, surrounded by his family. By then, the sixty-year-old Paulding had been married three times and had twenty-one children, four by his first wife, Sarah Teed of Salem, Westchester County, and the rest by his other two wives, Esther Ward[114] and Hester Denike, both from Peekskill. Many notables attended his burial service on February 20 and gave eulogies. Among them was his old comrade in arms, Isaac Van Wart. Twenty West Point cadets stood at attention and fired three volleys in honor of Patriot John. A life mask was done by the noted sculptor John Henri Isaac Browere who also did masks of Presidents Adams, Jefferson and Madison and General Lafayette.

Isaac Van Wart died nine years later in 1827 with similar pomp at his burial in the Dutch Reform Church Cemetery in Elmsford, New York.

In 1830 David Williams, the sole survivor of the famous trio, was honored on the fiftieth anniversary of the capture of André with parades and festive ceremonies. During a special anniversary performance of *The Glory of Columbia*, at the point in the play when the character portraying him was to speak his first line, Williams stood up in the audience and received a standing ovation. He was seventy-six years old. He died the following year and was buried with appropriate military pomp in Livingstonville, New York. In 1876, the one-hundredth anniversary of the Declaration of Independence, his body was moved to Old Stone Fort in Schoharie County just east of Albany. On that occasion a crowd of 10,000 turned out to celebrate the dedication of a large monument erected in his honor.

---

[113] Ibid., 46-47.

[114] This writer is a direct descendant of John and Esther's son, Caleb.

Life Mask of John Paulding
Fenimore Art Museum, Cooperstown, New York

— POSTSCRIPT —

A search for the few remnants of John Paulding's heroic legend as "the man who saved America" on that fateful day of September 23, 1780, has led to scarcely legible inscriptions on roadside and cemetery monuments, a tiny archival collection protected by a part-time librarian at a small historical museum in Tarrytown, seldom used historical archives at a few libraries and to the literary and artistic productions of once-famous American writers, painters and dramatists, now all but forgotten themselves.

In an age like ours when we eagerly—almost desperately—seek authentic, realistic, native-born heroes who are true to the American democratic heritage, none is more worth recovering and celebrating than John Paulding and few dates more worthy of remembrance than September 23, 1780.

— A P P E N D I X —

The Pauldings of the Hudson Valley

Joost

John Paulding's great grandfather, Joost (Joseph) Pauldnick, arrived in America from Cassant, Holland, in about 1680. A clothier, shoemaker and bolter by trade, he settled in New Amsterdam, where his Dutch forbears had first landed aboard the *Unity* and the *New Netherland* in 1624. The Dutch had been building homes and conducting successful businesses since 1626 when Peter Minuit famously purchased the island at the base of the Hudson River from a tribe of Algonquin Indians for trinkets valued at about 60 guilders or $24. They called the place "Manhattan," (Algonquin for "island of hills").

Although the mouth of the Hudson River had been discovered in 1524 by Giovanni Verrazano on behalf of Francis I of France, it was Henry Hudson sailing for the Dutch on the *Half Moon* in 1609 who first explored the river and made landings as far north as Albany. The river was to be called by various names before it finally immortalized the Dutch explorer: "Mannhatta" and "Shatemuc" by the local tribes, "Maurtius" after Prince Maurice of the Netherlands, "Great River of the Mountains" by Henry Hudson himself, the "North River" by early mariners and settlers who wished to distinguish it from the Delaware River to the south and the Connecticut to the east. In the years immediately following Hudson's exploration of "his" river, the number of Dutch fur trappers trading with Algonquin tribes along the river banks increased but there was no substantial settlement until 1614 when a village with fort and palisades was built at Fort Orange (Albany).

Thereafter, for much of the century Dutch settlers migrated southward even as new immigrants, like the Pauldniks, were arriving directly at the port in Manhattan. Before long the entire region along the river between the substantial settlements at Albany and New York City was populated, if thinly, by Dutch farmers, most of them working as tenants on the estates of the wealthy patroons. Any Dutchman who could gather at least fifty families could receive a grant from the West India Company for a large tract of land that he would own forever. The patroon was given almost absolute authority to rule his estate. This feudalistic system of colonization eventually failed because it discouraged the immigration of large numbers of those middle class, self-sufficient yeomen farmers and artisans necessary for successful settlement of a large area. The estates of the patroons also fell victim to increasing tensions between landlord and tenant and to the frequent raids from Native American tribes and vagabond elements among settlers who resented and coveted the wealth of these few families who controlled so much of the best land along the river. Only one of the great feudal estates, the Van Rensselaer, survived to the middle of the nineteenth century.[115]

Under the effective if autocratic and unpopular governorship of Peter Stuyvesant between 1647 and 1664, the prosperous Dutch colony of New Netherlands, comprising much of the Hudson Valley, grew to more than 6,000 souls living in New Amsterdam and in small settlements north of the city along both sides of the Hudson River. Because the Dutch West India Company, which had owned and ruled the colony since 1629 on behalf of the Dutch government, pursued an aggressive immigration policy that encouraged national and religious diversity, settlers came from all over Europe: Huguenots, like the Pauldnicks, from France; Calvinist Walloons from Belgium, Flemings from The Netherlands itself; Jews from Germany; Swedes; Norwegians; and of course, the English. The colony was the first example of the American "melting pot," a reflection of the characteristic climate

---

[115] For discussions of Dutch settlement and influence in the Hudson Valley, see Alice Kenney, *Stubborn for Liberty: The Dutch in New* York, New York, 1975, and John Mylod, *The Biography of a River: The People and Legends of the Hudson Valley*, New York, 1969.

of tolerance and inclusiveness that had made Holland the cultural and intellectual center of seventeenth century Europe. This second wave of "pilgrims" to America was very unlike the more narrow-minded, judgmental and exclusionist English Puritan "Pilgrim Fathers" who had settled a bit farther north just a few years earlier.[116]

The thickly wooded forests north of Manhattan were occupied principally by usually friendly Native Americans, along with many not-so-friendly wolves, bear and wildcats. Among tamer and more useful occupants of the area were abundant geese, turkey, nuts, wild cherry and apple trees and, of course, a river full of edible fish. The land itself, when cleared for farming, was fertile and productive. This new-found lower Hudson River Valley home of Joost Paulding and his family was, indeed, a promising area for settlement.

In September of 1664, less than twenty years before Joost Pauldnick's arrival, an English troop under the command of Richard Nicolls, acting for the Duke of York, easily conquered New Netherlands and governed it in the name of King James II. (The English claimed that John Cabot and John Smith had preceded Henry Hudson in discovering these shores and that the area rightly belonged to them.) The disaffected Dutch settlers offered little resistance, preferring English rule to the tyranny of Stuyvesant. The English renamed the territory and its major city, New York. They also anglicized the government and legal systems and established the Anglican Church. They did not, however, practice religious intolerance, economic discrimination or otherwise attempt to drive out Dutch settlers, including the prosperous patroons. The Dutch were still a dominant force in the life of New York when Joost Pauldnick arrived later in the century, although they were gradually moving further north on Manhattan Island and then up along the Hudson River all the way to Fort Orange. Even Governor Stuyvesant, who had fled to Holland after the English takeover, soon returned to his great farm

---

[116] A recent if somewhat overstated explication of the thesis that it was the Dutch and not the English who provided the characteristic openness and tolerance in American culture is Russell Shorto, *The Island at the Center of the World*, New York, 2004.

(*bowery)* at the southern end the island and was buried there in 1672 under his chapel on a site where St. Mark's Episcopal Church now stands.

Like most settlers of his day, Joost stayed on Governors Island for some time before crossing the East River to lower Manhattan. He was soon sharing in the prosperity of many of his Dutch neighbors. In addition to successfully plying his native trades, he engaged in merchant trading as an increasingly wealthy part-owner of a privateer named, appropriately enough, *Wheel of Fortune*.

The seventeenth century of Joost Paulding was the time of Dutch ascendancy in exploration and conquest, not only in America but all around the world. This was the era of Henry Hudson and the great Dutch East and West India Companies. This was also the golden age of Dutch art—the century of Rembrandt and Jan Vermeer. By the end of the century, William of Orange ruled England as well as Holland, and Dutch influence had spread throughout the globe leaving place names, institutions and political and cultural influences that have lasted for more than four hundred years. Nowhere was this impact more evident than in the area along the Hudson River stretching from its mouth in lower Manhattan Island some 150 miles north to Albany. In this region Dutch culture remained dominant well into the nineteenth century under the strong influence of powerful and influential families with names like Vanderbilt, Van Rensselear, Van Courtlandt, Vanderlyn, Roosevelt, Van Buren and many, many more. These families constituted a dominant group of businessmen, philanthropists and political leaders, including three American Presidents. Not least among the important Dutch families of the Hudson Valley were the descendants of Joost Pauldnick.

In 1683, Joost became a citizen of New York and five years later married a local Dutch woman named Catherine Duyts, with whom he had three sons and five daughters. Like the other early Dutch settlers, Joost moved into the dock areas along the lower East River and set up his artisan clothing and shoe shops in this busy business and shipping center, probably on Duke or Wall Streets. By the early eighteenth century, Dutch settlers were sharing the areas south of Wall Street with the more prosperous

English and French and gradually moving further north both in the center of the island and along both riverfronts.[117]

When Catherine died, Joost joined this Dutch migration and moved northward from the City to the small settlement of Tarrytown—then called Phillipsburg. In 1709 he married a widow living there named Zophia Krankeit. Thereafter, the prosperous Joost and his family moved back and forth between Manhattan and Tarrytown, keeping homes in both places. Travel was usually by river but land travel was increasingly possible as the English built a network of roads to replace the old Indian trails and the crude roadways of the Dutch. Before long, the great King's Highway, connecting most of the settlements in the Hudson Valley along both sides of the river all the way to Albany, was completed.

Joost's oldest son, Joost Jr., (c. 1710-1773) married Susannah White in New York City in 1732. Twenty years later the couple moved to a farm near Tarrytown with their family that included, at the time, three sons, Joseph (Joost) III, William and Peter, all of whom were to serve in the Revolutionary War. Son Joseph, although he would one day be the first Supervisor of Greenburgh Township, within which Tarrytown was located, was destined to be less prominent in American history than either his father or his younger brother, William, (1735-1825) or his son John (1758-1818).

William

William Paulding, like his father, was born and raised in New York City, but unlike his father, who settled down as a farmer outside Tarrytown, he ran away to sea as a young man and eventually made such a success in merchant trading that he commanded several ships sailing out of New York. In 1762 he returned to New York a rich man and married Catherine Ogden. Shortly thereafter, he moved to Tarrytown and built a large house and warehouse along the river. By the outbreak of the Revolution in 1776, William Paulding was one of the most prosperous and

---

[117] For maps and commentary on the area where the Pauldings settled, see Eric Hornberger, *The Historical Atlas of New York City*, New York, 1989, esp. pp.41, 56, and 62.

influential citizens in the lower Hudson Valley, profiting from the regular trade between the dock in front of his house and New York City. In that year he was elected as one of eleven delegates from Westchester County to the historic New York Provisional Congress meeting at White Plains. He cast his historic vote in favor of the Declaration of Independence and almost immediately thereafter accepted the critical post of commissar in the New York militia with the rank of colonel. Later in 1776, or sometime in 1777 after the Battle of White Plains, with the English army threatening Tarrytown, William moved his family north to safety in a family compound that he named Pleasant Valley, located near Millbrook in northern Putnam County, well behind the American lines.

As commissar for New York troops, William Paulding, like his counterparts in the other colonies, had the awful responsibility of supplying the American troops with necessary provisions, especially food. His was the thankless task of trying to persuade farmers to sell him their produce for what everyone knew was virtually worthless paper money issued by a weak government that had little cash, no good credit to back up what it had and no effective taxing power to raise necessary funds. When farmers refused to respond to his entreaties on behalf of hungry soldiers, the generous and patriotic Paulding paid for needed provisions out of his own pocket, drawing down on his considerable personal fortune.

After the war, William moved his family back to their substantial riverside home in Tarrytown. When the New York legislature and the national Congress both failed to reimburse him for his expenses, as promised, he was financially ruined and forced into debtors' prison in White Plains, the very town where he had affixed his signature to the Declaration of Independence less than a decade earlier. While he was held in jail, his Tarrytown mansion was seized and sold by creditors. After some time, the jail burned and Paulding, a deeply embittered man, simply walked out and went home to Catherine who had managed to keep the house after all by accepting a mortgage from the creditors.

Of William Paulding's seven surviving children, two made noteworthy contributions to American life. The most politically and socially prominent was William, Jr. (1770-1854), a successful lawyer and politician in New York City. This William became adjutant general of the state, was elected to a term in the U.S. Congress from 1811-1813 and served in the War of 1812 as a major general of New York militia. Always deeply involved in the political infighting of the day, first as a Democrat and later as a Republican, he wrote a letter in 1823, when he was the state's brigadier general of militia, accusing the Federalist Governor, DeWitt Clinton, of packing the officer corps in the state militia "in order to elevate his political friends, and to depress his Republican opponents" and "to place, as far as practicable, the military of this City under federal control."

Not long after penning this letter, Paulding changed parties and ran successfully as a Republican for two terms as mayor of New York between 1825 and 1829. One of the highlights of his mayoral tenure was the opportunity to entertain General Lafayette at his home in Greenwich Village during the French hero's triumphal return to America in 1827. Another pleasant duty that may have been even dearer to his heart came his way in the same year when he journeyed northward to St. Peter's Cemetery in Van Cortlandville, near Peekskill, to dedicate a memorial to his famous cousin, John, and to give a long speech heralding Patriot John as an American folk hero who had displayed great courage and sacrifice at a critical moment in the War for Independence.

William's most dramatic and enduring achievement is Lyndhurst, the magnificent riverside mansion at Tarrytown that still stands in all its glory as a National Trust Historic Site. Between 1836 and 1838 Paulding, then in his sixties and retired from public life, acquired 184 acres, including 1,300 feet of Hudson River frontage near Tarrytown. Here he built a retirement home just north of Sunnyside, the estate of family friend and writer, Washington Irving. A man of relatively simple tastes, Paulding nevertheless wished to live with his wife, Maria Rhinelander Paulding, and youngest son, twenty-year-old Philip, in fine style and to entertain his guests in a manner suitable to his high station in society. He called his home, simply, "Knoll" and employed the most talented architect of the day, Alexander Jackson Davis, to design the mansion and landscaping.

Davis was a part of the dominant romantic and naturalist artistic and philosophical schools of the day. He employed the nostalgic and picturesque gothic revival style that he felt blended the house well with its natural surroundings. He also made extensive use of large windows to let the natural beauty of the outdoors inside. He filled the landscape with linden and beech trees which are today among the largest and most magnificent of this species to be seen anywhere. The most striking part of the mansion is Paulding's library on the second floor of a magnificent gothic tower with huge windows that afford sweeping views of the river. The overall result was—and is—one of the most beautiful mansions in America, an appropriate memorial to one of the leading families of New York City and the Hudson Valley during the formative years of the country when this region and its people played such a vital role in its development.[118]

James Kirke

William's younger brother, James Kirke Paulding (1778-1860) was hardly less well-known than he. Born at the family hideaway at Millbrook during the war, James later became a friend and colleague of boyhood playmate and neighbor, famed writer Washington Irving, and of another renowned author of the day, James Fennimore Cooper. James' older sister, Julia, married Irving's brother, William, and the two families were close. James not only collaborated on some of Irving's work, especially the well-regarded satirical periodical *Salmagundi* that recounted the foibles of New York City life, but was also a literary pioneer in his own right. He was one of the first truly indigenous American writers with his incorporation of Native American and Dutch materials into his work. Like his father, James also made a considerable mark in public life. He was an active Jacksonian Democrat in both state and national politics and served as secretary of the navy under another Hudson Valley Dutchman, President Martin Van Buren.

---

[118] After Paulding's death in 1854, his mansion passed through other hands before finally becoming the property of New York financier and railroad magnet, Jay Gould, in 1880. Gould gave the property its present name, Lyndhurst. In 1961, the Gould family bequeathed the property to the National Trust for Historic Preservation.

James Paulding was aware that despite the fame and fortune of many of the Pauldings, including his own considerable reputation and that of his father and older brother, there was a poor cousin in the family tree who deserved more approbation for patriotic courage and impact on American history than any Paulding since his great grandfather Joost had first ventured across the ocean to Manhattan Island in the seventeenth century. Never mind that cousin John was a barely literate dirt farmer and was something of a hustler who had had to make his way during the difficult years of the Revolution by taking his opportunities where he could find them. When it counted, John had been a hero, perhaps the most important hero in the War of Independence.

And On

For the rest of the nineteenth and well into the twentieth century the Pauldings continued to be key figures in the history of the Hudson River Valley and the nation. In the generation after William, James and John, Hiram Paulding (b. 1797) was a rear admiral in the Civil War who commanded the Brooklyn Navy Yard, helped to develop the famed warship, the *Monitor* and was among those instrumental in opening up China to international trade. One of Hiram's sons, John C. Paulding (1832-1913), was the leading Republican figure in Peekskill in the days of Presidents Buchanan and Lincoln. For his political effectiveness and loyalty he was rewarded with the coveted patronage plum of inspector of customs for the Port of New York. Early twentieth-century Pauldings from Westchester and Dutchess Counties were leading business figures holding such positions as president and vice president of the New York Central Railroad and president of the prestigious Union League of New York.

But the accomplishments of all of these successful Pauldings combined did not equal the singular achievement of their poor relation, Patriot John.

PAULDING GENEALOGY
JOOST PAULDING TO PHILIP SECOR

JOOST PAULDNICK   -m- CATHERINE DUYTS
arr. America c.1680   b. 1644

JOSEPH PAULDING, JR -m- SUSANNAH WHITE
1710-1773

JOHN PAULDING   JOSEPH PAULDING II -m- SUSAN GARDINER   WILLIAM PAULDING
                  d. 1773   1735-1825

SARAH TIDD (1) -m- JOHN PAULDING   -m- ESTHER WARD (2)   WILLIAM   JAMES KIRKE
1761-1781   "PATRIOT JOHN"   1768-1804   PAULDING, JR   PAULDING
                                                            1770-1854   1778-1860
H. DEINIKE (3) -m-   1758-1818
d. 1865

HIRAM PAULDING   CALEB PAULDING   MARY PAULDING
b. 1797   1804-1890?   1812-1890

WILLIAM DEPEW PAULDING
1841-1895

EMMA PAULDING -m- RICHARD TUTTLE
1860-1936   1862-1919

GENEVA TUTTLE -m- JOSEPH EIBLE
1885-1945   1882-1944

WINIFRED EIBLE -m- ALLEN B. SECOR, JR.
1910-1995   1909-1984

PHILIP B. SECOR -m- ANNE L. SMITH
1931-   1932-

Drawn by Anne Secor

— BIBLIOGRAPHY —

Adams, Arthur. *The Hudson through the Years*. Westwood, New Jersey: 1983.

Aderman, Ralph M., ed. *The Letters of James Kirke Paulding*. Madison, Wisconsin: 1962.

Bailey, Anthony. *Major André A Novel*. New York: 1987.

Bakeless, John. *Turncoats, Traitors and Heroes*. New York: 1959.

Benson, Egbert. *Vindication of the Captors of Major André*. New York: (1817) 1865.

Boynton, Edward. *History of West Point and its Military Importance During the American Revolution*. New York: 1863.

Brown, R. "Three Forgotten Heroes." *American Heritage*, May, 1957.

Canning, J. and W. Buxton. *History of the Tarrytowns*. Harbor Hall Books, 1975.

Carmer, Carl. *The Hudson*. New York: 1989.

Cooper, James Fennimore, *The Spy: A Tale of the Neutral Ground* (1821), New York, 2002.

Diamont, Lincoln. *Chaining the Hudson: The Fight for the River in the American Revolution*. New York: 1989.

Drummer, H. "Major André's Captors: The Changing Perspective of History." *Westchester Historian*, vol. 75, Spring, 1999.

Dunlap, William. "The Glory of Columbia: Her Yeomanry," 1803 in Richard Moody, ed., *Dramas from the American Theatre 1762-1909*. New York: 1966.

————. *André: A Tragedy in Five Acts*. New York: 1798.

Flexner, James Thomas. "Benedict Arnold: How the Traitor Was Unmasked." *American Heritage*, August, 1975, 25-29.

PATRIOT JOHN

———. *The Traitor and the Spy.* Boston: 1975.

Hall, Charles Swain. *Benjamin Tallmadge: Revolutionary Soldier and American Businessman.* Columbia University Press, 1943.

Harr, John Ensor. *A Novel of Benedict Arnold and the American Revolution.* New York: 1999.

Herold, Amos L. *James Kirke Paulding: Versatile American.* New York: 1926.

Holmes, L. *David Williams and the Capture of Major André.* Schenectady, New York: 1926.

Hornberger, Eric. *The Historical Atlas of New York City.* New York: 1989.

Irving, Washington. *A History of New York* (1809). Boston: 1984.

Irving, Washington (with James Kirke Paulding). *Salmagundi or the Whim-Whams and Opinions of Launcelot Langstaff,* New York, 1807.

Jones, Thomas. *History of New York During the Revolution.* 2 vols., New York: (1788) 1879.

Karl, J. *Who Was Who During the Revolution.* Indianapolis: 1976.

Kenney, Alice. *Stubborn for Liberty: The Dutch in New York.* New York: 1975.

Koke, Richard. *Accomplice to Treason: Joshua Hett Smith and the Arnold Conspiracy.* New York: 1973.

Lossing, B. J. *Pictoral Fieldbook of the Revolution,* New York, 1851.

Martin, James Kirby, *Benedict Arnold Revolutionary Hero.* New York: 1997.

Meade, Rebecca Paulding. *The Life of Hiram Paulding.* New York: 1910.

Mylod, John. *The Biography of a River: The People and Legends of the Hudson Valley.* New York: 1969.

Nathans, Heather S. *Early American Theater from the Revolution to Thomas Jefferson.* Cambridge University Press: 2003.

Patterson, Emma L. *Peekskill in the American Revolution.* Peekskill, New York: 1944.

Paulding, James Kirke. *John Bull in America.* New York: 1825

———. *The Old Continental Or the Price of Liberty.* New York: 1844.

Paulding, William I. *Literary Life of James K. Paulding.* New York: 1867.

———, ed. *The Bulls and the Jonathans.* New York: 1867.

Pennypacker, Morton. *General Washington's Spies on Long Island and In New York.* Brooklyn: 1939.

Proceedings of a General Court Martial of the Line [trial of Benedict Arnold]. 1780.

Purcell, E., *Who Was Who in the Revolution*, New York, 1993.

Randall, William Stone. *Benedict Arnold Patriot and Traitor.* New York: 1990.

Raymond, M. *David Williams and the Capture of Major André.* (pamphlet), Tarrytown, New York: 1993.

Reynolds, Larry. *James Kirke Paulding.* Boston: 1984.

Rinaldi, Ann. *Finishing Becca: A Story About Peggy Shippen and Benedict Arnold.* New York: 1994.

Roe, Charles H. "André's Captors: A Study in Values." *Westchester Historian*, vol. 42, no. 4. 1966.

———. "The Paulding Family." *Westchester Historian*, vol. 43, #5. 1967.

———. "The Paulding Homestead at East View." *The Quarterly Review of the Westchester Historical Society*, July, 1934, #3, 58-61.

Smith, Joshua Hett. *An Authentic Narrative of the Causes Which Led to the Death of Major André.* 1801.

Sparks, Jared, ed. *The Correspondence of the American Revolution.* Boston: 1853.

————, *The Life and Career of Major André.* Boston: 1861.

————, *The Life and Treason of Benedict Arnold.* Boston: 1835.

————, *The Writings of George Washington.* Boston: 1834-37.

Stimpson, F. J., ed. *My Story: Being the Memoir of Benedict Arnold.* New York: 1917.

Tallmadge, Benjamin. *Memoir of Colonel Benjamin Tallmadge.* New York: 1858.

Van Doren, Carl. *Secret History of the American Revolution.* New York: 1941.

Wallace, Willard. *Traitorous Hero: The Life and Fortunes of Benedict Arnold.* New York: 1954.

Walsh, John. *The Execution of Major André.* New York: 2001.

Ward, Harry M. *Between the Lines.* New York: 2002.

Wilson, Barry K. *Benedict Arnold: A Traitor in Our Midst.* Montreal: 2001.

Wood, Christopher. *The War of the Revolution.* 2 vols., New York: 1952.

Wood, W. J. *Battles of the Revolutionary War.* Chapel Hill, NC: 1990.

— INDEX —

About the Author

Philip Secor has been an enthusiastic student of American political history since his high school days. At sixteen he spent a week in Washington as the prize for winning a state oratorical contest in American history. Later he taught politics at Duke University, and Dickinson and Davidson Colleges before serving as Dean of Muhlenberg College and President of Cornell College.

Secor is the author of six books, including a biography of another forgotten hero, Richard Hooker, the sixteenth century founder of the Anglican religious tradition. He lives with his wife, Anne, in eastern Pennsylvania.